Improving Children's Homework, Organization, and Planning Skills (HOPS)

NASP

NATIONAL ASSOCIATION OF
School Psychologists

By Joshua M. Langberg, PhD

A PARENT'S GUIDE

From the NASP Publications Board Operations Manual
The content of this document reflects the ideas and positions of the authors. The responsibility lies solely with the authors and editors and does not necessarily reflect the position or ideas of the National Association of School Psychologists.

Published by the National Association of School Psychologists

Copies may be ordered from:
NASP Publications
4340 East West Highway, Suite 402
Bethesda, MD 20814
301-657-0270
301-657-3127, fax
866-331-NASP, Toll Free
e-mail: *publications@naspweb.org*
www.nasponline.org/publications

Improving Children's Homework, Organization, and Planning Skills (HOPS): A Parent's Guide
ISBN: 978-0-932955-50-0

Printed in the United States of America

14 15 16 17 18 19 10 9 8 7 6 5 4 3 2 1

Table of Contents

Preface

The Homework, Organization, and Planning Skills (HOPS) intervention was developed collaboratively with school counselors and school psychologists; the treatment manual was published in 2011 by the National Association of School Psychologists (NASP). The HOPS intervention is now being used in many schools across the United States. The intervention was designed to be implemented by school mental health providers at school, during the school day, and it is most often implemented individually or in small groups. Multiple school districts have also started implementing parts of the intervention school-wide (e.g., the binder organization system). Implemented individually or in small-group format, the HOPS intervention can be completed in sixteen 20-minute meetings. HOPS is primarily used with middle school students but is also used with elementary and high school students.

After publishing the treatment manual, the school mental health providers implementing HOPS expressed interest in having a companion book directed toward parents so that they could work collaboratively with parents to support students' academic success. School mental health providers have limited time during the school day to work with students, and it is difficult for them to address behaviors that take place primarily in the home setting, such as homework completion. Further, they noted that when parents were highly involved in the process, improvements made through HOPS were more likely to be maintained across school years and transitions between schools. Accordingly, this parent version of HOPS was written with the hope that it will allow parents and school mental health providers to work together effectively to support academic success.

It is important to note that the term *parents* in this book is intended as a broad term and includes any person who takes responsibility for monitoring a child's behavior and supporting the child's success in school. As such, these interventions can be implemented by a parent or parents, grandparents, guardians, mentors, and older siblings. The key factor is whether the person is able to monitor and support the child's behavior on a consistent basis. For example, if the person is not regularly present in the child's environment after school, when homework is typically completed, it will be difficult to implement the homework completion intervention described in this book. However, some of the interventions, such as the binder organization and homework recording interventions, could be implemented by any adult who can commit to monitoring the child's progress with the intervention at least once every week. From this point forward, the term *parents* will be used to refer to any adult who has taken responsibility for consistently working with the child to improve homework, organization, and planning skills.

This book is not only for parents of children who are experiencing difficulties with homework, organization, and planning skills. The principles and interventions described in this book can be used to improve children's existing skills, and to teach children to implement skills more effectively or to use more advanced skills. All children need to learn to effectively organize their materials and time, because these skills remain important through college and into employment. Many children struggle to learn these skills and often learn them through a difficult process of trial and error. With the tools provided in this book, parents can support their children in learning these skills with the goals of preparing them for the years and transitions ahead.

The intervention section of this book provides parents with the tools to implement five separate homework, organization, and planning interventions, depending on their child's needs. These sections are followed by a chapter that provides information on collaborating with the school to improve students' homework, organization, and planning skills. Even if the school is not familiar with the HOPS interventions, parents can still be successful in working with their children, and doing so may open the door to new conversations and collaborations with the school. The next chapter provides real-life examples of families who have used the HOPS interventions and have overcome bumps and barriers along the way. Finally, the last chapter focuses on next steps, including what families can do if they have successfully implemented the HOPS interventions and are looking for additional ways to promote their child's academic success.

Acknowledgments

I want to thank my mentors, Steven W. Evans, PhD; Bradley H. Smith, PhD; and Jeffery N. Epstein, PhD, who taught me the importance of the guiding principles described in this book for helping children reach their full potential. I also want to thank my children, Kaitlin and Alexis, and my wife, Lisa, for supporting and encouraging me when my attempts to consistently follow the guiding principles fall short.

Introduction

Chapter 1

Overview: How to Use This Book

INTRODUCTION TO THE INTERVENTIONS AND THE GUIDING PRINCIPLES

This book includes a description of five different interventions. You can pick and choose the interventions you try, depending on your child's needs. However, it is important to note that all of the interventions presented in this book rely on the same guiding principles, or keys that are critical to changing and improving children's behavior. These overarching principles are described in Chapter 2, and it is strongly recommended that you read Chapter 2 before implementing any of the interventions. By reading Chapter 2 first you will (a) know why the strategies suggested are likely to work, (b) be better able to overcome obstacles and fine-tune the interventions more quickly, and (c) go into the intervention process with a realistic idea of how much work will be required of you and therefore be more likely to develop a realistic intervention plan.

As described in detail in Chapter 2, simultaneously targeting more than two behaviors for improvement is very difficult. Targeting multiple behaviors or skills at once is very time consuming for the parent who is implementing the interventions, and it can be confusing for the child. Accordingly, Chapter 2 encourages parents to set priorities and to start by seeking to improve those areas that they deem most important for the child's academic success. If you are working with someone else (e.g., a partner or spouse) to implement these interventions, it may be helpful for you each to rank the interventions in order of importance and then compare lists and come to an agreement on where to start. The next sections briefly summarize the contents of each intervention described in this book to help you begin to think about which intervention to start with.

HOMEWORK RECORDING

Chapter 3 focuses on improving how consistently and accurately children record homework assignments and tests. Many children have difficulty consistently recording homework assignments in their school planners. As a parent, you know that it can be extremely difficult to support your child's homework completion at home if you don't know exactly what needs to be accomplished and when assignments are due. Sometimes teachers help children with recording homework assignments, or parents are able to look online to see what the child needs to complete. However, you still might want your child to take more responsibility for accurately recording homework. This chapter provides strategies for promoting effective homework recording behaviors. This intervention would be a good place to start if you find that you are having daily battles with your child over what needs to be completed, or you are spending a lot of time trying to communicate with teachers to confirm what your child is expected to complete.

HOMEWORK COMPLETION

Chapter 4 focuses on improving the actual process of homework completion after school. In this chapter, you will learn strategies for structuring the homework environment, keeping your child on task and focused, and helping your child complete homework efficiently. The chapter also includes some strategies for helping your child to study more efficiently. This intervention would be a good place to start if the process of completing homework each night is stressful and often leads to negative interactions or arguments with your child. You might also consider starting with this intervention if homework completion time goes smoothly but is taking considerably more time than teachers suggest it should. For example, if homework is taking so long that your child is not going to bed on time, then this would be an important intervention to try.

ORGANIZATION OF MATERIALS

Chapter 5 focuses on interventions and strategies for helping children improve the way they organize their school materials and keep them organized. Typically, classwork and homework papers are organized and transferred to and from school using a school binder and a bookbag. For this reason, the chapter provides strategies for establishing and monitoring structured systems for binders and bookbags. For example, your child has dozens of styles of school binders to choose from at the beginning of the school year. Which binder might work best for him, and why? The chapter also discusses techniques to help your child maintain systems of organization once they are established. This ability is important because many students start off the year organized but then rapidly become disorganized. If your child frequently completes homework but then fails to turn it in, or if your child forgets to bring home the books and assignments needed to complete homework, this intervention would be a good one to start with. Also, if you open your child's bookbag and find many crumpled papers at the bottom (and perhaps some old food and clothing), this would be an important intervention for you to try.

PLANNING AHEAD TO COMPLETE SCHOOLWORK

Chapter 6 provides strategies for improving children's ability to plan ahead for the completion of schoolwork, including homework, tests, and long-term projects. Children tend to procrastinate and to put off homework until the last minute. This tendency can cause considerable family stress about work completion and can also lead to rushed completion of work, careless mistakes, and poor preparation for tests. Planning ahead to complete schoolwork is an advanced skill. Accordingly, this intervention would work best with students who are middle school age and older. This might be a good intervention to start with if your child regularly records and completes homework but procrastinates and is thus not able to demonstrate his academic potential on tests. This would also be a good intervention for parents who have been supporting their child's planning activities and want to see him take more responsibility for planning ahead to complete work. For example, parents often want to begin teaching their child to take more responsibility for planning ahead because they anticipate transitions to high school and college, where parental support is more difficult to provide. This intervention can be used to transfer the responsibility for planning ahead from you to your child.

MANAGING TIME AND BALANCING RESPONSIBILTIES

Chapter 7 focuses on strategies and interventions to help children balance school and extracurricular responsibilities by teaching them to estimate how much time activities are likely to take and when they would best be accomplished during the week. This intervention is often implemented together with the planning intervention described in Chapter 6, or after those planning skills have been mastered. For example, if the child has planned ahead and specified that he is going to study flashcards for 30 minutes, the next step would be to think about when would be the best time to study, taking into consideration all the other activities that need to be completed after school. This intervention might be a good place to start if you have an adolescent who has a busy after-school schedule and has difficulty balancing school and extracurricular activities.

DECIDING WHERE TO START INTERVENTIONS

Often, children who have significant problems in one area are likely to have problems in other areas too. This can make it difficult for families to choose where to start their interventions. As noted above and as discussed in detail in the next chapter, it is best to start by targeting one or two skills (i.e., by implementing one or two interventions).

Ask yourself the following questions as part of your decision process:

1. If implemented perfectly, which skill would affect my child's grades the most?
2. If implemented perfectly, which skill would reduce our family's stress the most?
3. In terms of negative interactions with my child, which of these behaviors and skills is our family most frequently talking or arguing about?

COLLABORATION: WORKING WITH YOUR CHILD'S SCHOOL

Chapter 8 discusses the importance of gathering teacher input before you decide which intervention to start with, because teachers may be able to offer a unique perspective about which skills are most important for your child's academic success. Also, by contacting your child's school, you will find out whether or not the school is already providing interventions that target some of these homework and planning skills and whether or not your child is making progress as a result. For example, if a school mental health provider at your child's school is already focusing on organization of school materials and your child is making significant improvements, then you might want to focus your efforts on time management and planning. Alternatively, if a school mental health provider is focusing on organization and your child has been slow to respond, then it may be most beneficial for you to work collaboratively with the school mental health provider and to monitor and reward organization at home to support your child's progress. Sometimes parents need to gather more information before determining if the skills they are asking their child to work on are developmentally appropriate. Chapter 8 recommends that parents schedule a meeting with their child's teachers, school counselors, and school psychologist to discuss HOPS before they start implementing interventions. Teachers and counselors, who have the benefit of seeing many different same-age children, are good sources for knowing what would be developmentally appropriate expectations for your child.

EXAMPLES OF SUCCESSFUL INTERVENTION SYSTEMS

Chapter 9 provides two real life examples of families that have implemented the HOPS interventions. The term *real life* refers to the fact that sometimes implementing the interventions doesn't go exactly as planned and adjustments need to be made. The family in the first example implemented the homework recording (Chapter 3) and the organization of materials (Chapter 5) interventions. Specifically, in this example, the parents of a sixth-grade student are implementing the teacher initials and bookbag and binder organization systems. The family in the second example implemented the planning ahead (Chapter 6) and balancing responsibilities (Chapter 7) interventions. In this example, the parents of a ninth-grade student are having their child use her planner to plan in advance for the completion of assignments, tests, and projects, and to use evening schedules to outline when those activities will occur during the day or week. As you will see in both of these examples, the parents initially had difficulty adhering to some of the guiding principles outlined in Chapter 2, and as a result, the interventions got off to a rough start. However, both of these families were able to make adjustments to how they were implementing the interventions and ended up with successful intervention systems.

CHOOSING NEXT STEPS

The final chapter in this book (Chapter 10) provides suggestions for parents whose children continue to struggle academically even after the HOPS interventions have been implemented. As noted in Chapter 10, children can experience academic difficulties for a wide variety of reasons, and not all of those reasons are addressed by the HOPS interventions. The chapter includes a table that is designed to help you begin to identify other aspects of your child's behavior that may be contributing to her academic difficulties. The chapter then provides recommendations for where you can seek out further assessment and intervention that will address the identified areas of weakness.

Chapter 2

Guiding Principles for Improving Behavior

Listed below are the guiding principles for improving children's behavior and teaching them new skills. The principles, which follow the acronym FAMILY, are defined and discussed in detail in this chapter. There is a direct positive relationship between the number of principles you follow and the progress your child will make with the interventions described in this book, with greater progress resulting from each additional principle that you follow.

FAMILY

1. **Feasibility**—Providing effective intervention is hard work for parents. Start small so that you can implement the intervention exactly how you intended.
2. **Achievable goals**—Set easy-to-achieve goals for your child to ensure that he has success early in the process. You can always raise the bar later.
3. **Monitoring and rewarding**—The intervention simply will not work if the child's progress with homework, organization, and planning skills is not consistently and frequently monitored and rewarded.
4. **Intervention should be fun**—The tone you set with your child when discussing why you are implementing an intervention and how it will work is very important. Set a positive tone, making it clear that this is an opportunity for the child.
5. **Letting go**—Picking your battles, focusing on your child's successes, and temporarily letting go of the other concerns you have about your child's behavior will make the intervention process go more smoothly.
6. **You**—You as the parent are a critical piece of the puzzle. You need to monitor your own stress level and seek help if necessary to ensure that personal issues do not get in the way of your child's success.

Feasibility

Implementing interventions not only is work for the child (learning new skills) but also is work for the parents. Helping children to improve their homework, organization, and planning skills means that parents must check in (monitor), track (physically record), and reward behavior consistently and frequently, which takes considerable time and effort. For example, as outlined in Chapter 4, to improve your child's homework completion behaviors, you may monitor and record whether or not your child is on task and working as frequently as once every minute during homework time. Similarly, as outlined in Chapter 3, to ensure that your child is recording homework consistently and accurately, you will need to check her planner every day after school and record her progress. An unfortunate fact about asking children to learn new skills or behaviors is that if progress is not tracked and monitored consistently, the chances for improvement are slim. Frequent monitoring and tracking are time consuming, and the more behaviors you are trying to address at once, the more difficult the process gets. For these reasons, you should pick one or two behaviors to target initially for intervention. Monitor whether or not you are able to implement the intervention consistently and follow the other guiding principles. If the answer is yes, go ahead and add additional interventions.

Achievable Goals

Many children tend to get frustrated and to give up quickly when things are not going their way. This is especially true for children who have experienced what they perceive as a series of previous failures. Children who are struggling in school are often bombarded by adults telling them that they need to do better, suggesting how they should do better, and offering rewards for improvement. Unfortunately, for a variety of reasons, prior attempts to help probably have not been very successful, and as a result, children get frustrated and adopt a "Why try?" attitude. This is actually a perfectly understandable attitude to take when you consider your own life or work situation. Let's say that your boss frequently tells you about areas that you need to improve at work and sets up plans for you to meet certain targets. You put in considerable effort to achieve the targets but are not successful. Now let's say that this happens over and over. How would you respond the next time your boss gave you feedback and introduced a new target? Perhaps with some choice words mumbled under your breath or with some eye rolling? This is why it is important for children to experience success soon after starting with the HOPS interventions. Otherwise, they may quickly feel discouraged and stop trying to meet the goals and targets you have established (see Chapter 9, "Liza," for a real life example of this).

By establishing achievable goals for your child, you can ensure that she has some success early in the intervention process and is therefore motivated to continue trying. In training programs, psychologists learn that, if necessary, you should "praise a child for breathing well." This essentially means that you need to find a way for your child to have some success and to feel good about what she is doing, no matter how small, so that she remains engaged. In the context of the HOPS interventions, this could mean setting an initial goal of the child simply bringing home her school planner, rather than immediately focusing on how many assignments she recorded. Or you might set an initial goal of writing down *something* in her planner related to homework each day of the week (rather than immediately focusing on the accuracy or details of what is recorded). When your child accomplishes these small goals and you say "Good job! You did it, and here is your reward," she will probably look at you in stunned silence. The key is that she will then be motivated to take the next step and meet a slightly higher goal.

Monitoring and Rewarding

Monitoring and rewarding are probably the most important principles in ensuring that your intervention efforts are successful. As such, prepare yourself for the longest section in this chapter. If you do not consistently monitor and reward your child's efforts, he may make improvements initially, but those gains will likely drop off over time. This is because many of the other guiding principles depend on consistent monitoring. For example, you can't set achievable goals unless you first monitor your child closely to establish a realistic target. You also won't know if the intervention is feasible until you are monitoring at the suggested level and frequency. Finally, you can't provide praise and rewards at the right times unless you are consistently monitoring your child's progress. Below, the importance of consistent monitoring is discussed in detail, followed by a section focused on why it is important to use rewards to motivate your child and the types of rewards that work best.

Monitoring

For the HOPS intervention, *monitoring* means physically recording (writing down), at an established frequency, whether or not a certain behavior occurs. An example is reviewing your child's school planner every day after school and recording on a tracking sheet how many assignments he wrote down and how many assignments he was expected to write down (number of classes he had that day). Another example of a monitoring plan could be recording on a tracking sheet how many minutes during a 15-minute period a child was on task (looking at homework or writing) while completing a math assignment. The hitch with monitoring is that if it is not done with the agreed-upon frequency (i.e., every day or every minute in the examples above), the child will stop trying. Essentially, the child starts to think, "If Mom or Dad isn't going to check, then I can get away with not doing it," or "If Mom or Dad can't even check when they said they would check, why should I keep doing this?" This is where monitoring ties back into the principle of feasibility. Essentially, if you don't currently have the time to monitor and track consistently, then it is better to wait to provide the intervention until you do have time. If you monitor inconsistently or less frequently than you stated that you would, then your child will end up with a negative experience, making it less likely that he will try in the future.

Why Use Rewards?

Once parents establish a system for consistently and frequently monitoring their child's behavior, it becomes easy to link the child's performance (whether or not he is achieving his goals) with rewards. You may already know that the use of rewards with children is sometimes controversial. Everyone has a different opinion of whether or not rewards should be used and what types of rewards are okay. In this book, the term *reward* is used very broadly and is meant to represent anything that you as a parent do or say that makes the child more likely to want to complete the behavior again in the future (e.g., record homework). Rewarding your child can be as simple as giving a pat on the back or saying "Nice job, I am proud of you." Rewards can also refer to earned privileges or material items (e.g., extra time outside or a new video game). From time to time, a promise to remove monitoring works as a reward. For example, "If you are able to record your homework for every class this week, then I will stop checking your planner every day and will check it only once, at random, during the week." This works as a reward because many children (especially adolescents) dislike being closely monitored.

In this book, parents are primarily encouraged to use verbal praise and privileges as rewards. Privileges refer to those activities that your child finds fun and engages in on a daily basis (or would like to), including, but not limited to, watching television, staying up 30 minutes past bedtime, picking what is for dinner or dessert, going to a friend's house after school, playing video games, and spending time on a cell phone. None of these activities costs money, and when a parent thinks creatively like this, the list of potential rewards is almost endless. The reason that verbal praise and privileges are emphasized in this book is that they can be provided frequently, that is, on a daily basis, which is important for ensuring that your child remains motivated. For example, let's say that you tell your child that she can earn a reward at the end of the week (e.g., she can go to a movie with friends) if she records her homework assignments every day that week. If your child forgets to record her homework once (e.g., on Tuesday), the opportunity to earn a reward is now gone and, as such, she has no motivation to record her homework on the remaining days that week. Rewards work best when they are available *daily,* as children will inevitably make mistakes and need to have the opportunity to quickly turn things around and to do better the next day. Further, if rewards are provided daily, children can be rewarded for their success repeatedly, which builds confidence and increases the likelihood that they will continue to work to meet the goals you establish.

A common concern with the use of rewards is that parents will have to keep providing rewards forever to get their child to continue to complete tasks. Sometimes parents also feel that they should not have to be providing rewards for "things the child should be doing anyway." These are important issues to address, as they may get in the way of the intervention being effective. To start off, ask yourself whether you would go to work and put in your best effort if you didn't like your job and didn't get paid. This may seem like a silly question, but many children struggling in school are actually in a similar position. They do not like school, do not enjoy the tasks they are being asked to do, and do not get paid (rewarded) for their efforts. Why would anyone expect children who experience school this way to work hard? The only reason children might work to improve their homework, organization, and planning skills is if they are internally motivated to do so, if they just know it is the right thing to do or in their best interest and are driven to succeed.

Indeed, for most parents, seeing that their child is internally motivated to perform well at school is the ultimate goal. However, this raises two questions: First, if your child is not currently internally motivated, why not? And second, where does internal motivation come from? The answer to the second question is that internal motivation often comes from experiencing success and the positive feelings that you associate with success. Experiencing success leads to the desire to experience those positive feelings again (i.e., the internal motivation). Many children who can benefit from the HOPS interventions do not experience success very often (at least not related to homework, organization, and planning), they do not feel good about their school performance, and they have low confidence in their chances of succeeding in the future. It is not reasonable to assume that children who feel this way will be internally motivated to put effort toward improving their homework, organization, and planning skills.

Going back to the original parental concern of "Will I have to keep providing rewards forever?" the answer, fortunately, is no. In HOPS interventions, rewards are used to allow your child to experience success, to jump-start the process of learning to work for something, so that internal motivation can take hold. However, it is important to be realistic and to recognize that all people work for rewards, so in a sense, the answer is still no, you will not always have to provide rewards, but your child will always be working because there are rewards available (e.g., a paycheck or feelings of satisfaction). Often, those with concerns about rewards feel better when a broader definition of rewards is used and when one accepts that rewards are simply a natural part of life and important to all people.

Using Point Systems and Reward Menus

In many of the interventions described in this book, children earn points for implementing skills. For example, a child might earn one point for every homework assignment recorded correctly. Points are then accumulated and can be saved up and traded for rewards. It is often helpful if the child has a choice of rewards rather than a single reward option. This is because children will frequently get tired of or bored with the process if there is only a single reward and may become less motivated to continue using the skills. Having options to choose from helps the rewards stay interesting and meaningful. Remember, if the rewards are not meaningful (if the child really does not care if he gets them or not), they will not work.

In multiple places in this book it is suggested that you create a reward menu, that is, a list of rewards, with different point values for each reward. Reward menus tend to work best when they contain mostly immediate or short-term reward options that can be used on a daily basis. Sometimes, reward menus also contain longer-term options that the child can save up points to earn. Developing a good reward menu can be difficult, but it is a very important part of having a successful intervention experience. Make the process fun by working with your child to develop the menu and options, and then negotiate how many points each item should be worth.

An example of a reward menu is provided in Figure 2.1. The point values listed next to each reward should be based on how many points the child is realistically expected to receive daily (remember, set the bar low). This example is for a child who receives one point for each homework assignment he records accurately and in sufficient detail. Assume that this is the first week of the intervention and that previously the child was recording assignments but doing so inconsistently. In this example, the child is in middle school and has four core classes (math, language arts, social studies, and science), so he is expected to have four things written down every day (the child must write "no homework" if none was assigned). The child should be able to earn a

FIGURE 2.1. **Example Reward Menu**

Reward	Point Value
20 extra minutes of video game time	2
20 extra minutes of TV time	2
Go to bed 20 minutes later	2
Eat dinner in front of the TV	3
Use Mom's cell phone for 20 minutes	3
Pick out what's for dinner	4

reward (have some success) daily during the first week to make sure he is motivated to continue recording assignments. Accordingly, some rewards on the example menu are worth two points, so if the child records two assignments out of four, he earns something. Remember, later you can and will raise the point total the child needs to earn to get a reward.

This reward menu is just an example; you do not have to use these same reward options with your child. One important factor for determining what rewards go on the menu is what you as the parent are comfortable with. For example, you may not ever want your child eating dinner in front of the television, so you would not include that as an option. The key take-home point is that the child in this example can earn a small reward daily so that he experiences success quickly, and so that when he makes a mistake (this is bound to happen), he will still have a reason to be motivated to try the next day. Also, remember that the rewards need to be meaningful, so in the above example, if the child was already allowed 3 hours of screen time per day, an extra 20 minutes might not be worth much to him. This is why it is important to take time to consider what privileges your child already has access to before establishing your reward menu.

Some children, or more often adolescents, may find saving for big-ticket items more motivating and meaningful. In this case, it is fine to create a reward menu that includes both short-term immediately available reward options and long-term, delayed options that the child has to save for. Figure 2.2 is another example of a reward menu, revised to include some longer-term (delayed) options.

Tracking Points

When your child is earning points, being consistent in how you record the points earned is very important. Recording of points really needs to be done on paper, because failure to do so leads to parent–child disagreements and prevents the parent from making informed changes to the child's goals over time.

FIGURE 2.2. **Example Reward Menu, Including Delayed Reward Options**

Reward	Point Value
20 extra minutes of video game time	2
20 extra minutes of TV time	2
Go to bed 20 minutes later	2
Rent and watch a movie	8
Receive money to go to the movies with friends	12
Pick the place for family dinner out	8
Go bowling with Dad	12

FIGURE 2.3. Example of Point Tracking Sheet

	DATE				
	10/7	10/8	10/9	10/10	10/11
Homework recording	0	0	13	7	
School binder	3	4	7	9	
Points earned today	3	4	20	16	
Total points in bank	**3**	**7**	**27**	**33**	
Total points used	**0**	**0**	**10**		

Note. In this example, the child had 27 points in the bank on 10/9 and used 10 points, leaving him with 17 points. On 10/10 he earned 16 more points and so his total points in bank is now 33 (17 + 16).

Specifically, unless you physically record points, you will not be able to detect trends. Trends (either upward or downward) are used to determine when it is time to make changes to the intervention. For example, if your child records an average of two homework assignments each day over a 2-week period and occasionally records three, then it is likely time to raise the bar, such as making the smallest reward on the menu worth three points. If you do not consistently record and monitor the points your child earns each day, it will be very difficult to make these types of decisions. In addition, your child will be motivated by being able to see the points he has earned and the progress he is making over time. For example, you may want to post the sheet you use to track points in a place where your child can see it, such as stuck to the refrigerator with a magnet. Having the point tracking sheet in view will also remind you to monitor your child's use of the skills each day. If your child is enjoying the intervention and having some successes, he will likely start coming to you and reminding you to complete the tracking sheet because he will be looking forward to showing you his progress. Finally, you should physically record points because you need to keep a running total of accumulated points so that your child has the opportunity to save, or bank, points. Tracking sheets do not need to be complicated; you simply need a piece of paper much like your child's school planner, with dates going across the top row and the name of the behaviors you are tracking listed down the first column. The example provided in Figure 2.3 shows a tracking sheet where the child is saving points. If the child uses points (trades them in for a reward), the amount used is subtracted from the total points, and the points remaining are recorded on the sheet.

Intervention Should Be Fun

Have you ever attended a presentation or a workshop or listened to your boss introduce a new initiative at work? If so, you would probably agree that the delivery of the material matters a great deal in terms of how the message is received. Some presenters are exciting and could hold your attention for hours while delivering a talk on the rate grass grows in different climates. Other presenters have new, innovative, and fascinating ideas, but everyone in the room is checking their e-mail or "listening" with their eyes closed. What does this have to do with the HOPS intervention? How you introduce the HOPS intervention to your child really makes a difference in how she receives the message.

Read these two introductions to HOPS interventions and see which you think would work better.

"You have not been doing well in school. You missed five homework assignments last week and are in danger of failing math. It is completely unacceptable that you don't write down your homework every day! This is a task that any middle school student can do. From now on, your father and I are going to check your planner each day after school to see whether or not you recorded homework assignments. If you have not, there will be no TV or video games that day after school. Do you understand?"

"Your teachers are really assigning tons of homework this year. Your dad and I can barely keep up with all the different due dates for homework, tests, and projects. We know you are really working hard to get things in on time and want to reward you for your efforts. For the next 2 weeks, your dad and I are going to check your planner each evening to see whether you have recorded your homework assignments. We want you to record your assignments legibly and in enough detail that we can tell exactly what needs to be done and when, including dates and page numbers. Your dad and I are going to check with your teachers every day to see if what you recorded is accurate. We will then provide you with rewards each day after school, depending on how many assignments you recorded accurately. Why don't we sit down together and make a list of potential rewards you might like. We can include things like extra TV time or a later bedtime, or even picking the desserts we have after dinner. What do you think?"

These two scenarios described similar interventions that link homework recording to privileges. Which approach will result in complaining and arguing, and which might result in passive agreement, such as "Fine," or "Okay, I guess"? Presentation matters, and it is equally important to maintain this positive tone during the process of implementing the intervention. As much as possible within your own personality and style, try to be your child's cheerleader while she is learning to use her new skills. The trick is to focus on the positive. For example, let's say that your child comes home tomorrow and has recorded assignments for three out of her four classes. Let's also say that her baseline (before intervention) was to record zero or one assignment per day. You could say, "Great job! You recorded three assignments. Would you like to take your TV time now or later?" Alternatively, you could say, "Good job recording three assignments. Which class did you miss? Math. Okay, why did you miss math? Let's talk about that. What can you do better next time to get your math assignment recorded? You know you have a D in math, don't you?"

Do you think the child in the second example even heard the praise, or did the negative statement drown it out? The child in the first example might be willing to give homework recording another try the next day and might think "This new system is okay after all." The child in the second example would likely think, "Here we go again, I tried and it wasn't good enough. I messed up as usual." That child is highly unlikely to put more effort into homework recording.

This is not to say that you won't have to give your child feedback or suggestions for improvement along the way. You most certainly will. However, if you have focused on the positive throughout, these pieces of constructive criticism will be easier to deliver and more likely to be well received (without lengthy argument). When providing your child with feedback, you might want to try what is known as a *praise sandwich*. First, say something positive, such as "We know you have been working hard and have made progress this year." Then provide the feedback or instruction, for example, "I really want you to make an effort to record your math assignment tomorrow," followed by more praise: "Keep up the good work!" This technique will help you to maintain an overall positive tone while also communicating that there is more work to be done.

Letting Go

Earlier, this chapter discussed the difficulty and ineffectiveness of trying to address many different behaviors at the same time. This chapter also noted the importance of focusing on the positive whenever possible to help your child stay engaged and motivated. The principle of letting go means you may have to temporarily ignore some of your concerns about your child's behavior in order to maintain a positive focus on the specific behaviors you are targeting. This is often called *picking your battles*.

Continuing with the homework recording example above, assume that the child in the example has difficulty keeping his room clean and sometimes gets reports sent home from school saying that he talks too much with peers during class. The child comes home with three out of four assignments recorded, and the parent says,

"Yes, I see that you recorded your assignments. Good job, but tell me about this talking out in class comment in your planner. What were you thinking? How many times have I told you not to talk during class? Also, I need you to go upstairs and clean your room, because as usual you didn't listen when I told you this morning." This is a parent who is having trouble letting go of the other issues the child is struggling with, and as a result, the positive focus on homework recording is completely lost. Take a moment and put yourself in this child's shoes and think about how the above interaction would feel. Would you feel good about your progress with homework recording? Would you be motivated to record your homework the next day at school? Letting go is hard. It is often difficult because parents so badly want to see their child succeed in all areas. Your ability to let go is directly related to the final principle reviewed below, "You."

You

Think about all of the principles that you have just read about and ask yourself if you would be able to accomplish them if you were feeling stressed and overwhelmed (being a cheerleader, having a positive attitude and approach, and letting go). This is not to suggest that you should or can magically stop feeling stressed. The important point here is to *acknowledge* how your own stressful feelings or feelings of sadness or depression might get in the way of you working effectively with your child. Although you cannot make your stress disappear, everyone's level of stress and their mood naturally fluctuate throughout the day. The goal is to attempt to interact with your child about the HOPS intervention during those periods when you are feeling best, because this will allow you to work more effectively with your child. The reverse is also true. Try to avoid bringing up topics related to your child's homework, organization, and planning skills when you are feeling stressed or are in the midst of a negative interaction with your child about a different topic.

Some parents find it helpful to plan ahead and to schedule their HOPS intervention discussions with their children. For example, you might check the planner or school binder for organization at the same time each afternoon or evening. This routine not only helps your child quickly learn what is expected, but also is an opportunity for you to plan ahead for the interaction and to take a few deep breaths to reduce your stress level. Sometimes all you need is a 5-minute break to then be more focused and effective when you speak with your child. In addition, many parents find it helpful to write out a script ahead of time with what they want to say to their child. For example, you might write out the "praise sandwich" you want to deliver before going into the interaction. In some cases, life is currently too stressful to effectively implement any of the suggestions outlined above. If that is the case for you, consider seeking help and additional support to formally address your stress level and mental health. It is better to do nothing (provide no intervention) than to implement an intervention that is going to lead to a negative experience for your child, because every time an intervention isn't a positive experience, she is less likely to engage in future attempts.

TROUBLESHOOTING

If, when you move on to implement some of the interventions outlined in this book, you find that you are struggling and feel that your child is not making progress, remember the acronym FAMILY and take time to review the guiding principles again. It may help to ask yourself the following questions:

1. Feasibility—Have I taken on too much at once?
2. Achievable goals—Is the bar set too high? Is my child having some successes?
3. Monitoring and rewarding—Am I monitoring consistently? Am I keeping up my end of the bargain? Do I have meaningful rewards in place?
4. Intervention should be fun—Am I approaching the intervention and my interactions with my child positively? Am I showing enthusiasm about my child's progress?

5. **Letting go**—Do I spend more time talking to my child about what she is doing well or about the things she needs to improve? If the latter, what can I let go of so that the scale tips to the positive?

6. **You**—Am I talking to my child about the intervention when I am feeling my best? Are my own stresses and difficulties getting in the way of doing my best with this intervention?

Interventions

Chapter 3

Homework Recording

SUMMARY OF THE INTERVENTION

The overall goal of the intervention is to:

- Improve the frequency and consistency with which children accurately record homework assignments in their school planners.

What is needed to implement this intervention?

- A school planner, sometimes called a schedule book or an agenda.
- A layout in the planner with the days of the week and dates across the top row, with a separate space beneath each date for the child to record homework assignments for each of his core classes.

What is required of you, the parent?

- Willingness to check the child's planner every day after school and to record on a tracking sheet how many assignments or teacher initials the child receives.
- Willingness to establish a reward menu as outlined in Chapter 2, making the child's daily privileges contingent on whether or not the homework was recorded accurately.

Developmental considerations:

- Most children are not expected to record homework assignments in a planner until at least the third grade, and they would likely still need prompting from a teacher until fifth grade.
- Once a child is in fifth grade, it is reasonable to expect that he can record homework assignments in a planner consistently and without prompting.

BACKGROUND

With multiple teachers assigning homework, quizzes, tests, and long-term projects, ensuring that your child is consistently and accurately recording assignments becomes critical during the middle school years. Students in elementary school are sometimes able to get by without writing assignments down by relying on memory. However, in middle school, students quickly learn that the strategy of just remembering what homework is due no longer works. Furthermore, during this period, children often start increasing their efforts to deceive their parents regarding homework assignments. Students quickly learn that when a parent asks if they have any homework, if they say no, it means that they get to go outside and play. Parents often don't find out that assignments are being missed and tests are not being adequately prepared for until it is too late. But some parents go to great lengths to figure out what homework is actually being assigned each night. Parents gather information about assignments and tests in the following ways:

- E-mail the teacher
- Call the teacher
- Use a teacher-provided weekly outline of the curriculum that lists assignments
- Go to a website that lists homework assignments and upcoming tests
- Call a phone system through which the teacher updates homework assignments

Each of these alternatives requires a significant amount of parental effort or is not 100% reliable. For example, even when phone or website systems are in place, they may not be updated consistently by some teachers. Furthermore, teachers are often forced to deviate from curriculum and assignment outlines (e.g., for a snow day or assembly), and the homework information becomes inaccurate. Finally, finding common times for parents and teachers to communicate daily about homework assignments requires a significant amount of time and effort.

It is important for parents to be able to quickly determine exactly what homework their child has been assigned each day. After all, you can't support your child in completing her homework after school if you don't know what needs to be completed. Unfortunately, many parents find that they cannot easily figure out what was assigned on a daily basis. For this reason, the intervention described in this chapter involves having the child ask the teacher to initial in the planner that homework assignments are recorded correctly. However, for parents who can determine what was assigned on a daily basis with minimal effort (e.g., through an online system that is consistently updated), simply monitoring and tracking the number of assignments recorded in their child's planner (rather than the number of initials received) and checking the online system daily to see if what was recorded is accurate, is sufficient.

DESCRIPTION OF THE INTERVENTION

For the teacher initials intervention, parents ask their child to record homework assignments for each class, and then to have teachers check and initial that the recording is accurate. If the child has no homework, he is expected to write the words "no homework" and have the teacher initial that. This way, after school, when parents check the planner, they can quickly determine what homework was assigned that day. If the child has four core classes every day, as is often the case in middle school, there should be four teacher initials in the planner every day.

The following are a few important points for parents regarding the teacher initials intervention. First, it is often helpful for parents to meet with their child's teachers to discuss the rationale for the intervention and to ask whether the teachers would be willing to initial the planner each day (i.e., rather than just telling the child to approach his teachers and ask them to initial the planner). Second, it is important for parents to emphasize to their child and teachers that getting teacher initials is the child's responsibility. Teachers will be more likely to receive the request positively if you stress that it is your child's responsibility to ask for initials at a convenient time. You could ask the teacher to suggest what time and method would work best. For example, some teachers request that the child record his homework and then leave his planner open and out on the corner of his desk so that they can initial the planner when it is convenient. Other teachers would prefer that the child bring her planner up to them at the end of class. Third, your child is not going to need to get initials for the entire school year, and you can tell the teacher that you will be phasing out the collecting of teacher initials as your child learns to record homework accurately (described in the next section). Teachers are often more willing to put the effort into reviewing and initialing the planner when they know that the task is temporary.

PHASES OF THE INTERVENTION

The teacher initials system is implemented in two phases, based on the principle of *freedom through responsibility*. Specifically, if a child demonstrates responsibility for obtaining teacher initials daily for a set period of time (Phase 1), he earns the freedom of no longer needing to get initials (Phase 2). You determine when your child can stop asking the teacher to initial her planner by setting a specific goal. For example, you might tell your child that if she receives an average of at least three out of four initials daily over a 2-week period, then she can stop getting initials. Once your child enters Phase 2, you should check randomly with teachers (at least once per week) to ensure that your child is continuing to accurately record homework assignments. For example, you could photocopy a page of your child's assignment notebook and show it to the teacher once each week to document accuracy. Another option is to e-mail the teacher or to check the online system, if available. Parents should inform their child that if there is a discrepancy between what is recorded in the planner and what the teacher says was assigned, the intervention will go back to Phase 1 (initials) until the goal for moving to Phase 2 is again met.

MONITORING COLLECTION OF TEACHER INITIALS

The next step is for parents to establish a routine for checking their child's planner each day after school. It helps everyone to remember if the time is the same each day (e.g., immediately after you get home from work or right before dinner). Children receive one point for every teacher initial received (or each assignment recorded in Phase 2). A child with four core classes each school day has the opportunity to earn 20 points per week (i.e., four points per school day for five days = 20 points). As described in Chapter 2, parents record points on a tracking sheet and establish a reward menu. If you are concerned that your child may try to forge his teachers' initials, you should check in with your child's teachers occasionally to make sure the initials are genuine.

INTRODUCING THE TEACHER INITIALS SYSTEM TO YOUR CHILD

Below is an example script to use as a guide for introducing the teacher initials intervention to your child. Feel free to add details and to modify the script as needed.

Wow, you have been getting lots of homework this year! I can't keep all of the assignments and due dates straight. I see that you are putting lots of great effort into managing and completing your homework. I want to help you succeed, and I have a system I want you to try. With this system, you'll have a chance to earn some rewards. For the next few weeks I want you to have all of your main teachers—math, science, history, and language arts—put their initials in your assignment notebook next to the homework assignments you record. That way we will both know exactly what has been assigned and can work together to make sure nothing slips through the cracks.

During each class period I want you to record your homework assignments and then to have your teacher initial next to what you recorded. If you don't have any homework that day, just write "no homework" and have your teacher initial it. Your teachers can initial really fast as you are walking out of class. I already talked to your teachers about this and they know you are going to be asking. If you get these teacher initials consistently, you will only have to get initials for a few weeks. This is going to be temporary, just to get us on the right track.

One benefit of the teacher initials system is that I will know that everything you recorded is accurate and I won't have to bug you about it anymore. The main benefit for you is the points. You will be earning points for getting initials, and you can trade these points for rewards from a reward menu we will develop together.

You will earn one point for every teacher initial that you receive. I will be checking your assignment book each day, meaning that you can earn 20 points per week for getting teacher initials. This means you will start earning rewards fast! What do you think? How about we start thinking about things you would like to earn and we can put them on your reward menu? I know you are always asking to play video games after school and I am always saying no. Maybe that could be something to put on your reward menu?

LONG-TERM VIEW

Most children forget to record homework now and then and might bounce back and forth from Phase 1 to Phase 2 a few times before learning to record homework consistently. Stay positive and make sure that your child knows that forgetting is not a big deal and that she can move back into Phase 2 quickly. If your child seems to have the hang of recording homework (e.g., has been in Phase 2 for a month), you may want to consider moving on to another intervention. Specifically, you may want to stop providing points for homework recording and instead provide points for your child learning a different skill. If you decide to move to another skill, consider celebrating with a special meal or a special reward (e.g., family movie night). Tell your child that he has graduated and that you want to give him the opportunity to earn more points for a different activity (e.g., organization).

Chapter 4

Homework Completion

SUMMARY OF THE INTERVENTION

The overall goal of the intervention is to:

- Improve the amount of time children spend on task and focused when working on their homework so that they are completing work more efficiently.

What is needed to implement this intervention?

- No physical materials needed.

What is required of you, the parent?

- Willingness to closely monitor your child's homework completion time after school and to frequently record whether or not she is on task.
- Willingness to set specific and achievable goals for homework task completion each day after school.
- Willingness to establish a reward menu as outlined in Chapter 2, making the child's privileges contingent on her on-task behaviors and task completion.

Developmental considerations:

- The National Education Association suggests that approximately 10 minutes of homework per day per grade is appropriate. This means that parents could reasonably expect a third-grade student to be completing 30 minutes of homework each night and a sixth-grade student to be completing 1 hour of homework each night.
- How much support parents will need to provide their child to keep him on task during homework completion varies as a function of the child's grade in school. Parents could expect a third-grade student to have multiple questions about how to complete work and to seek guidance often. Parents could also expect that a third-grade student would have difficulty remaining on task and focused for longer than 20 minutes and might need a break at that point. In contrast, a seventh-grade student should be able to work more independently (ask fewer questions) and be able to work for an hour without taking a break.

BACKGROUND

Chapter 3 described the teacher initials intervention that is designed to help parents determine what homework their child has to accomplish each day after school. However, even when parents feel comfortable that they know what was assigned, there is still the monumental task of ensuring that all of the work gets completed in a timely manner. Parents often struggle with finding a balance between providing too much homework support (doing homework for the child) and providing too little (allowing the child to go to school without work completed). Unfortunately, homework time after school often leads to arguments between parents and their child about when work should be completed, how long she should study, how much work she should complete, and how accurate or error free the work needs to be before it can be turned in. Many children have multiple after-school commitments, such as sports practice or music lessons, leaving less time to do homework. Parents may find that completing homework takes their child well past an ideal bedtime and, as a result, she may have difficulty waking up in the morning. One parent summed up this issue of balance by saying, "I don't want to do all this, but if I don't he will fail, and I can't let that happen." The interventions described on the following pages are designed to help parents to effectively structure homework completion time, to increase the amount of time their child spends working effectively, and to reduce the number of negative interactions they have with their child about homework.

DESCRIPTION OF THE INTERVENTION

The homework completion intervention consists of three separate steps: (a) developing a homework routine, (b) defining and monitoring on-task behavior, and (c) setting specific and achievable homework completion goals. At the end of this chapter you should be able to establish a clear and consistent homework completion plan with your child that will define *when* and *where* homework will be completed each day, *what* behaviors are expected during homework time, and *how* your child will know when he has adequately completed his work. The three steps of the homework completion intervention are reviewed below.

Developing a Homework Routine

Most children work best when routines and structure are in place (even if they tell their parents the opposite), and having a consistent routine for homework completion will reduce the frequency of arguments. Many arguments arise when a child wasn't expecting some demand, and as such she views the demand as not fair. For example, the child wasn't expecting to have to start homework right away after school when she didn't have to the previous day. The child reacts by pushing back to see how far she can get by complaining and begging to finish her favorite TV show first, or start homework after dinner, or go to a friend's house to complete her homework. Children are very good at coming up with compelling reasons for putting off homework. Sometimes parents give in, and as a result the child is considerably more likely to engage in these behaviors (complaining and arguing) again in the future. When the homework routine is as close as possible to being identical every day of the week and parents consistently enforce the routine, the child begins to learn that pushing back, bargaining, and complaining are not effective, and she stops engaging in these behaviors.

For these reasons, parents are encouraged to establish a consistent homework routine that includes: (a) the amount of time devoted to homework every day after school is the same (irrespective of whether the child has homework), (b) the time of day when homework will be completed is the same, and (c) the location in the house where homework will be completed each day does not change. Ideally, this homework routine would be written down and posted in a public place in the house, as this also reduces arguments and misunderstandings.

For middle school students, it is recommended that parents designate 1 hour per day after school for completing homework. This number might be lower for elementary students and would likely be higher for upper middle school to high school students. Having 1 hour set aside for homework completion each day helps children learn good habits, such as completing a little bit of work each night rather than procrastinating and leaving work until the last minute. It also reduces arguments about whether the child has homework that night, because he always has 1 hour scheduled for schoolwork. For example, even if teachers did not assign work to be completed and turned in the next day, the child could still study for an upcoming test; or she could make flashcards or write and study the definitions from the most recent chapter in her textbook or handout (there will be a test eventually). In some cases, children will go to great lengths to convince their parents that they really don't have anything they can work on during the hour. For those cases, parents need to have grade-level worksheets ready for the child to complete. Or the child could complete a certain number of math problems or could read a story and answer questions about what she read. Grade-level worksheets can be printed for free from multiple websites (e.g., http://www.interventioncentral.org).

Although ideally homework time would occur at the same time after school each day, this is not always possible. Children and their siblings have extracurricular activities that may affect when they have time to complete homework. To work with extracurricular demands, a family schedule should be created that lists all of the activities that need to be accomplished each day after school. Then the parent and child can agree in advance on a time that the 1-hour homework period will fit each day of the week. Once this schedule is established, it is critically important that the parent follow the schedule closely. As described in detail in Chapter 2, when an intervention is implemented (in this case a schedule) and not adhered to, the child starts to think that the parent is not serious about the intervention and that he doesn't really have to follow the rules. Also, following the schedule some days and not others will most certainly lead to arguments. Children may initially resist the 1-hour mandatory homework time. In those cases, you are encouraged to give the schedule a try for at least 2 weeks. Typically, the first week is full of grumbling and complaining, but by the end of the second week, your child will have settled in nicely. If she sees that she can't convince you to yield, she will start to get comfortable with the predictability of the routine.

Once parents have established a consistent homework routine for their child, by making a weekly schedule and having him do homework daily, they need to address the child's actual process of completing homework. That is, the child needs to be able to stay focused for extended periods of time to make the most out of the designated homework completion period. Accordingly, the remaining sections in this chapter focus on strategies you can use to encourage your child to stay focused during homework completion and to work efficiently.

Establishing a Location for Homework Completion

In order to maximize the chances that your child will be able to focus during work completion, you will need to find a place in the home that has few distractions and is convenient for you to frequently monitor his progress (e.g., every 5 minutes). Oftentimes, the kitchen or the dining room table works well as the location for homework completion. Allowing the child to complete homework in his own room is not recommended. Minimizing distractions during homework completion time is very important. However, doing so often is not easy, because all family members need to be involved and to agree to house rules for homework time. For example, if your child can see the TV from where he is working, then the TV should not be turned on, even if other family members do not have homework to complete. Similarly, if your child is completing work in the dining room, his siblings should not be allowed to race through the dining room chasing each other or to play games where he can see them. Efforts to minimize distractions often work best when parents establish rules for the entire house for the 1-hour homework period. That way the child you are starting the intervention with doesn't feel as if he is being singled out or punished. For example, between 4:00 and 5:00 in the afternoon, anyone watching TV or playing needs to be upstairs. The only activities allowed downstairs are quiet activities such as reading or homework.

Defining and Monitoring On-Task Behavior

The next step in ensuring that your child stays focused during homework completion is defining exactly what behaviors you expect to see when homework is being completed. Failure to establish specific definitions about what behaviors are expected during homework time leads to arguments (e.g., "I was working hard!"). The following definition is recommended: The child is physically looking at a textbook, worksheet, or flashcards or is in the process of recording an answer. Once a definition is established, the parent should establish a consistent schedule for monitoring the child's behavior to see if he is meeting the definition. For children who have a difficult time staying focused during work completion, no longer than 5 minutes should pass in between parent observations of behavior. As discussed a little later, whatever the interval you decide on, that also will be the basis for giving your child points for paying attention to her work.

Parents should provide specific praise while monitoring their child's on-task behavior. For example, each time you record that your child is on task, you could say something like the following:

- Great job working hard on your assignment.
- You are really doing an excellent job staying focused.
- Wow, I really appreciate how hard you are working.
- I noticed that you checked your work and caught an error. That was great!
- Wow, you are really flying through that assignment. Keep up the good work!

Children should not be penalized for fidgeting and do not need to stay in their seats as long as they are meeting the definition of on-task behavior (e.g., a student could be pacing around the room but still reading from flashcards and reciting definitions). However, when a child is not on-task, the parent should clearly state that he is off-task and the reason why. For example, "I couldn't give you a point because were doodling on your worksheet." Or, "Sorry, you didn't earn a point that time because you had your head down on the desk and were not writing anything with your pencil." The parent should follow up these explanations for why a point was not awarded with a statement of encouragement whenever possible. For example, "I couldn't give you a point because you were drawing. Let's see if you can try really hard to focus so that I can give you a point next time I check. You are really close to your goal!" Most of the time, these types of redirection statements will suffice, and the parent will not need to issue commands like "You need to get started working right now!"

As described in Chapter 2, you should record the points your child earns—in this case for meeting the definition of on task when you check—on a tracking sheet in a way that is visible to your child. Seeing her points recorded for being on task is motivating. Instead of using a tracking sheet, some parents like to place pennies or other objects (paperclips, pompoms, etc.) in a jar on the table where the child is working. This allows the child to really see how well he is doing. Some parents report that verbal praise distracts their child. In those situations, the parent can rely entirely on placing objects that represent points into a jar that the child can see, because doing so takes the place of verbal praise.

Parents are also encouraged to use bonus points to promote motivation and engagement. For example, your child starts his homework time in a bad mood, with his head down for the first 7 minutes. You could offer five bonus points if the child can "turn it around" and be on task during the next 5-minute interval task the next time you check. Parents also can set specific on-task goals and allow their child to earn bonus points if he meets those goals. For example, let's say that during the first week of intervention your child averages being on task 50% of the time during a 60-minute homework period (i.e., on-task half of the times you checked). You could use this information to set a goal for the following week. For example, "If you can stay on-task for 75% of the time today I will give you 10 bonus points at the end of your homework completion time."

Setting Specific and Achievable Homework Completion Goals

Often parents find that they are arguing with their child over how much work needs to be completed and about what it means when the child says she is "done with" her homework. This disagreement over terms frequently occurs in the context of studying for tests. For example, the child goes upstairs and studies for 30 minutes and then says, "I am done; can I go outside now?" The parent quizzes the child and feels that the child doesn't know the material well enough and sends him back upstairs to study more. The child feels that this is unfair and responds, "You said I only had to study for 30 minutes!" These types of situations can be avoided by setting specific, carefully defined goals for what it means to complete each homework task.

Whenever possible, parents should have the child's studying efforts result in a written product. Most commonly, these written products are flashcards or outlines of textbook chapters or other assigned texts. Having a written product that the child presents to a parent when studying is completed reduces the likelihood that parents and children will disagree about expectations. For example, the parent might state: "Make 20 flashcards from the bold words in Chapter 5 of your social studies text with the word on the front and the definition on the back. You can be finished studying when you have made 20 flashcards and know at least 10 when I quiz you." The child may not like what she is being asked to do, but at least what is expected is clear. Similarly, when a child is completing a worksheet, parents should set clear goals for the number of problems the child needs to complete and how accurate her work needs to be. For example, "You can be done when you have completed 20 of the math problems on your worksheet, and when I check them and at least 15 are correct." As outlined in Chapter 2, setting realistic, achievable goals is critical; otherwise the child will not be motivated to work toward those goals.

Rewarding On-Task Behavior and Goal Attainment

Once parents have established specific definitions for on-task behavior and specific goals for task completion, it becomes easy to tie completion of these goals to rewards. How to implement a point system has already been discussed briefly. For example, the child could earn one point each time you check and he is on task. Those accumulated points could then purchase items or privileges from a reward menu. Parents also might want to offer bonus points for on-task behavior to help motivate the child. For example, you might tell your child, "If you are on task at least four of the next five times I check, you will earn 10 bonus points." You can also incorporate task completion goals into the point system. For example, "If you are on-task for at least half the time (e.g., 30 minutes out of a 60-minute period) and have completed at least 20 of your 30 math problems correctly, then you will earn 20 bonus points!" As discussed in Chapter 2, the points your child is earning can easily be linked with privileges. For example, if the child earns 20 points she can go outside or watch her favorite TV show. For more information on how to use rewards, see Chapter 2.

How Much Help Should I Provide?

Ideally, parents never physically complete work for their child. Specifically, a parent should avoid erasing or writing on their child's homework assignments and should not give him an answer before he has fully attempted to solve the problem and has come up with his own solution. In general, all assistance provided by parents should be child driven. For example, you might decide that you will not comment on whether your child's answers are correct unless she specifically asks you to. Your role is primarily to keep your child consistently focused and working by monitoring his on-task behavior and setting task completion goals. If he asks, "Did I get this problem right?" you are certainly allowed to answer yes or no. However, you should try to wait until your child has tried in earnest to complete the problem and has recorded an answer before you offer suggestions or intervene.

LONG-TERM VIEW

Over time, it may be possible to drop one or two of the three homework completion intervention components, that is, developing a homework routine, defining and monitoring on-task behavior, and setting specific and achievable homework completion goals. As with all the interventions described in this book, this section recommends providing children with the opportunity to earn freedom (parents reduce homework monitoring and structure) by demonstrating responsibility (they consistently meet the goals that parents establish). It is highly recommended that before reducing monitoring and structure, you have a threshold and a clear plan in place for what would trigger needing to put that monitoring step back in place. For example, your child really doesn't like having you monitor his on-task behavior during homework time. He says he can get his work done "without you treating me like a baby." You could establish a goal that you will stop monitoring on-task behavior as long as he continues to meet the task completion goals and is in bed by 9:30 p.m. In this scenario, you are allowing the child the freedom to monitor his own on-task behaviors and telling him that it is okay if homework takes longer as a result. Alternatively, you could tell him that he no longer has to complete 1 hour of work every day (regardless of what was assigned) as long as he doesn't miss more than one homework assignment over the next 2-week period. If he misses more than one assignment, the original system would be put back into place. In this way you can taper the level of structure and monitoring you are providing, while making sure that he can succeed before you completely remove that support.

Chapter 5

Organization of Materials

SUMMARY OF THE INTERVENTION

The overall goal of the intervention is to:

- Develop a structured organization system designed to help the child effectively transfer homework and school materials to and from school.

What is needed to implement this intervention?

- One 3-inch D-ring binder.
- Five or six folders that have inside pockets and that are three-hole punched.
- One packet of three-hole-punched dividers (typically, five or six per packet).
- One pencil and pen pouch that is three-hole punched.
- One packet of loose-leaf paper.

What is required of you, the parent?

- Willingness to check your child's school binder and bookbag two times per week using an organizational skills checklist to monitor how he is maintaining the structured organization system.
- Willingness to establish a reward menu as outlined in Chapter 2, for which the child earns points based on her adherence to the organization system.

Developmental considerations:

- Children are typically not ready to take responsibility for organizing their materials independently until the third or fourth grade.
- Children in grades 3–5 will need more frequent parent and teacher support to help them stay organized once a system is established, whereas children in grades 6–12 should be able to maintain their organization systems independently.

BACKGROUND

Around the transition to middle school, many children begin to struggle with keeping all of their papers organized and with successfully transferring materials to and from school each day. Often children arrive at home without the materials they need for completing their homework. Children may even complete their homework but then fail to bring it back to school. Poor organization can also lead to low test grades because children don't have the necessary materials to study from or don't know which materials are current (e.g., chapter outlines, study guides, or worksheets). This can be very frustrating for parents who want to help their child study effectively but can't because they don't know what their child needs to study and where those materials are located. This chapter presents a structured binder and bookbag organization system along with a suggested plan for consistently monitoring children's use of the system. By implementing and monitoring a structured binder and bookbag organization system, you can significantly improve the likelihood that your child will have all of the materials she needs after school and will turn in completed assignments.

As shown in the intervention description below, it is suggested that children use one binder for managing all class materials, with separate sections in the binder for each class. The rationale for suggesting a one-binder system is simple: the more binders, notebooks, and folders a child tries to maintain separately, the greater the likelihood that materials will get lost or forgotten. With the one-binder system, your child will have everything she needs for class at all times. That said, the binder system allows for flexibility, and many children have successfully used two, or even three, separate binders. For example, flexibility is sometimes necessary when teachers require the use of a class-specific organizational system, such as a separate binder or notebook specifically for science class. If teachers are hesitant about your child adopting the HOPS single-binder system, you might suggest to the teacher a 1-month trial period, with the expectation that if your child's organizational skills do not improve, she will go back to using the teacher's system. If a teacher is unwilling to allow your child to use the one-binder system, you may be able to work with the teacher to reach a compromise. For example, your child may be able to keep a separate notebook for science class (or a journal for language arts class) within her school binder so that all materials are still within a single binder. As with all of the interventions described in this book, it is the structure and the consistent and frequent monitoring and rewarding that lead to improvements, and these can be accomplished with multiple binders if necessary.

DESCRIPTION OF THE INTERVENTION

Having a specific and clearly defined structure for the binder materials will allow parents to consistently monitor and reward their child for keeping everything in order. If parents' instructions are not explicit, then it is difficult to come to an agreement about what being organized means.

Materials in the binder should appear in the following order:

1. Pen and pencil pouch
2. School planner
3. Homework folder (with pockets) labeled "Homework to be completed" on the left and "Homework to be turned in" on the right
4. Dividers with tabs to identify the class name (one for each class)
5. Folders labeled with class names (one for each class)
6. Loose-leaf paper (some in each class section for taking notes)

Securing the planner (where the child records homework assignments) within the three-ring binder will reduce the likelihood that it will get lost or left at school. The homework folder is a place for your child to keep all his homework assignments that need to be completed and turned in. The folder should be secured in the binder. Homework to be completed goes in the left side of the folder. Homework to be turned in goes in the right side of the folder. Attaching a label to the inside corners of the folder will help your child remember which side to put homework to turn in and which side to put homework to complete. Old homework papers (those that have been completed) should not be in the homework folder. Those need to be transferred from the homework folder to the appropriate class section folder.

Knowing What Materials to Purchase

Not all binders and folders are created equal. For some reason, children seem to be experts at accidently damaging binders. For example, binder rings quickly get bent out of shape, and folders and papers get ripped and start falling out. Plastic folders are recommended because they are nearly impossible to rip. The more expensive 3-inch binders (about $15 each) last longer because they are made so that the rings open easily (the child needs to press on only the top or bottom tab and the rings pop open). Having to use only one tab is surprisingly important because children open binders in a hurry and rarely take the time to put pressure on two tabs simultaneously, resulting in bent rings.

Setting Up the New Binder System

Parents should work with their child to transfer materials from the child's old binder system into her new binder system because this can be a large task. When tackling this with your child, you are encouraged to use a three-pile system: papers that clearly need to be thrown out, papers of uncertain value, and papers that clearly need to be kept and filed in the appropriate class section. You can then put all papers from uncertain pile in a folder and have your child go through the folder with one or more of his teachers.

Introducing the Organization System to Your Child

Below is an example of how parents might introduce the binder organization system to their child in a positive manner.

You really are getting lots of homework and classwork this year. It seems difficult to keep up with it all. I would like us to try organizing your materials a specific way this year. The new system may take some getting used to at first, but I think eventually you will find that it is easy to use. I have all new school binders, folders, and other materials for you to set up your new system. When we get your new system set up, we will talk about the rewards you can earn for keeping everything organized.

Once we have finished organizing your binder you will automatically meet all of the criteria on this organizational skills checklist. Then I will check in twice a week to see how you are doing with maintaining your organization system using the checklist. You will earn points for staying organized according to the definitions on the checklist. The more criteria you meet on this checklist, the more points you will earn. We can work together now to create a rewards menu listing items that you can earn using the organization points.

Monitoring the Binder and Bookbag

Once parents help their child establish the new binder system and clean out her bookbag, they need to put a consistent monitoring plan in place. Specifically, you should decide how often you will check to see if your child is staying organized and what specific criteria you will use to evaluate your child's progress. The recommended frequency for you to evaluate your child's binder and bookbag organization is at least once per week. Initially, you may find it very helpful to monitor twice per week because this rate ensures that your child does not fall too

FIGURE 5.1. **Example Organizational Skills Checklist**

	10/2	10/5	10/8	10/11	10/14	10/17
There are no loose papers in the binder.	YES/NO	YES/NO	YES/NO	YES/NO	YES/NO	YES/NO
There are no loose papers in the bookbag.	YES/NO	YES/NO	YES/NO	YES/NO	YES/NO	YES/NO
Homework to be completed is in the left side of the homework folder.	YES/NO	YES/NO	YES/NO	YES/NO	YES/NO	YES/NO
Homework to be turned in is in the right side of the homework folder.	YES/NO	YES/NO	YES/NO	YES/NO	YES/NO	YES/NO
Only current homework papers are in the homework folder.	YES/NO	YES/NO	YES/NO	YES/NO	YES/NO	YES/NO
Only papers that the child still needs are in the binder.	YES/NO	YES/NO	YES/NO	YES/NO	YES/NO	YES/NO
Total organization points earned today						
Total organization points earned overall (bank)						

far behind with organization. The organizational skills checklist (Figure 5.1) lists criteria that have been used in HOPS research studies to determine if a child is staying organized. You can add additional criteria or remove criteria that may not be relevant for your child's system.

Establishing a Specific Plan for Maintaining the Materials Organization System

Children rarely have established routines for making sure that their school binder and bookbag stay organized. The most frequently used strategy is to stuff loose papers into the bookbag until someone (parent or teacher) discovers the papers and makes the child do something about them. To be successful with this organization intervention, your child will need to develop a routine for staying organized. Initially, you should work with your child to help him develop a plan for monitoring his binder and bookbag organization, to ensure that he is prepared for when you will be completing the checklist.

To remain organized, your child will probably need to file and throw away papers at least once a week. You can work with him to create a specific plan to accomplish this by asking him the following questions and recording the answers.

• When (day or date, and time) will your child clean up his bookbag and binder?
• Where will the cleanup occur?
• What exactly is he expected to do/accomplish during the cleanup?
• How will he remember to complete the cleanup?

Have your child take the lead on generating ideas for maintaining his organization system so that he feels ownership of the process. For example, he might decide that he is going to go through and organize the papers in his binder and bookbag each Sunday night to get ready for the next school week. If your child is going to organize his materials on Sunday, it would be good for you to check his binder and bookbag using the checklist on Monday. This increases the likelihood that he will be prepared, be successful, and be rewarded for his self-management efforts. You are encouraged to establish a bonus reward for your child remembering on his own to complete the weekly binder and bookbag cleanup. For example, you might offer 20 bonus points the first time your child follows his self-management cleanup plan and as a result meets all the criteria on your organizational skills checklist. Providing your child with a copy of the organizational skills checklist allows him to consult the checklist during his own weekly cleanup. Sometimes children like to put a copy of the checklist in their room or in their binder.

LONG-TERM VIEW

The primary long-term goal of this intervention is to be able to remove the parent from the organization process. That is, the parent will be able to stop completing the checklist for the child's organization system, and the child will be able to manage and maintain his own bookbag and binder. In past research with the HOPS intervention, this has been accomplished gradually. Specifically, the parent sets a specific goal (e.g., at least five of the six criteria on the checklist are met for 2 weeks), and when the child reaches that goal, the parent reduces the frequency of monitoring (e.g., from two times per week to once per week). If the child meets that same goal for another 2 weeks, the parent stops checking altogether. However, the parent still continues to provide points for the child's own weekly binder and bookbag cleanups. Specifically, the child comes to the parent after he has organized his own materials and the parent takes a brief look at the binder and bookbag (checks for loose papers) and gives the child points for continuing to self-manage the cleanup process. You can continue to check in this manner for the entire school year to make sure your child is maintaining the system and to see whether any materials (binder or folders) need to be replaced. The points that your child was earning when you were completing the checklist can then be offered for using a new skill, such as planning ahead to complete schoolwork.

Chapter 6

Planning Ahead to Complete Schoolwork

SUMMARY OF THE INTERVENTION

The overall goals of the intervention are to:

- Reduce procrastination by improving children's ability to plan ahead for completing schoolwork and studying for tests.
- Teach children to break assignments and studying into smaller, more manageable pieces, and to designate specific times to complete each piece in advance of due dates.

What is needed to implement this intervention?

- A school planner, sometimes called a schedule book or an agenda.
- A layout in the planner with the days of the week and dates across the top row, with a separate space beneath each date for the child to record homework assignments for each core class. (Note: Some adolescents may be using electronic planners, that is, a calendar or schedule on a phone or one that is associated with an e-mail account. Limitations that should be considered are discussed later in this chapter.)

What is required of you, the parent?

- Willingness to work patiently with your child to gradually teach her how to plan ahead and to complete work in advance of due dates.
- Willingness to establish a reward menu, as outlined in Chapter 2, that will provide incentives for your child to use her schedule or calendar to plan out tasks in advance.

Developmental considerations:

- It is not developmentally appropriate to expect children in kindergarten through fourth grade to independently plan ahead for completing homework and studying for tests. You may work with children this age to start teaching them planning skills but should not expect them to implement the planning skills on their own.

- Children in 5th–7th grades can be expected to take on some planning responsibilities independently. However, parents will likely initially need to help their child refine his planning abilities for 1–2 months as well as provide further support.
- Students in 7th–12th grades can be expected to plan ahead for completing homework and studying independently. However, several weeks of practice will be needed before students in this age range fully understand the HOPS system and are able to implement the skills without parent support.

BACKGROUND

During middle school and continuing into high school, children's workloads (homework, projects, and tests) significantly increase. Also during this period, children start receiving larger comprehensive tests (sometimes called exams) that evaluate knowledge accumulated over extended periods of time, such as midterm exams covering all the material taught up to that point in the semester. At some point, children find that they can no longer be successful academically by dealing with tasks as they arise on a day-to-day basis. Children who are unable to plan ahead will eventually have too much work to complete in a given day, or at a minimum they will not have the time to devote sufficient attention and effort to all of the tasks at hand. Unfortunately, often it is when a child experiences failure, such as getting a D on a midterm after studying the night before, that alerts parents and children to the fact that study methods that worked for the child before are no longer sufficient.

When children wait until the last minute to complete work, it can be a very frustrating experience for parents. Parents often ask with exasperation, "Why didn't you tell me this yesterday when I had time to help you?" or "What do you mean you have a 10-page paper due tomorrow?" or "What do you mean you need a poster board tonight? I don't think the store is even open this late." The key to not completely losing your cool in these circumstances is to try to keep two things in mind. First, there is very little natural incentive for children to plan ahead (why would they?). Consider the choices your child is faced with on a daily basis after school: "I completed my homework and there is still an hour of daylight. I can go outside and play basketball, or I can stay in and get a head start studying for my test on Friday." Is it really reasonable to assume that a middle school age child in that situation will choose to stay in and study? What is the incentive for your child to study? Yes, you could argue that the incentive is that they won't have to study as much on Friday and might get a better grade on the test. The problem is, those rewards are far in the future, and children almost always choose the immediately available reward (going outside now) over the delayed reward (maybe getting a better grade on a test). That is why an important part of the intervention described below asks you to provide the incentive of an immediately available reward for your child when he engages in planning behaviors.

The second thing to keep in mind is that, although planning ahead sounds simple, children often have very little idea what planning ahead actually means and how to go about it. Specifically, children may acknowledge that waiting until the last minute to study is a bad idea, but they don't necessarily know when during the week they should study, how many times, for how long, or even how. Planning ahead and managing time are advanced developmental skills, and learning them is most often accomplished through a process of trial and error. Planning ahead requires students not only to understand what to do (study more in advance of the test), but also, and perhaps more important, to be able to monitor and track their own planning efforts and to make adjustments based on whether those efforts succeed or fail.

For example, a child who has a test on Friday might decide to study 20 minutes on Wednesday and 30 minutes on Thursday. If after following that study plan the child gets a C on the test, he needs to be able to evaluate and adjust if he wants to receive a higher grade. Perhaps next time he will study longer, or he might choose to start studying further in advance, or he might decide to try a different study method. Making these adjustments is necessary for success, but doing so is a complex process and a learned skill that many adults continue to refine over time. Accordingly, it is important for you to go into the planning intervention described below acknowledging that it might take some time before your child figures out how to effectively plan and complete work ahead of deadlines. However, planning skills are critical for academic success, and what you teach your child now will serve as the foundation that will allow him to continually evaluate his efforts and make improvements into the future.

DESCRIPTION OF THE INTERVENTION

In this intervention, parents can help their child learn to manage increasingly complex school assignments. Improving children's ability to plan ahead for completing schoolwork and studying for tests can reduce procrastination and give children greater control. Parents can help by teaching their child to break down assignments, projects, and tests into smaller pieces and steps and to plan when he will complete each task. The first step in implementing this intervention is to determine where your child should record her study and work completion plans.

In research that was done using this planning intervention, children would break down assignments and tests into small pieces and then record each task in a planner, under the date that they planned to complete the task. For example, if a child wrote "Math test" in the Friday space of his planner, then in the Thursday space of that week he might also write "Study math flashcards for 20 minutes." A paper-based planner works best in this scenario because everything is written in the same place and the child has access to his planner at school when tests and projects are announced. Some children have shown that they can successfully use electronic calendars to plan ahead. The downside is that children likely will not have access to electronic calendars at school (unless they have a personal computer in the class), and so the extra step of transferring the information from the school planner to the electronic one is necessary. The benefit of using an electronic calendar is that parents can set reminders and can overlay the child's planned weekly schedule with their own.

As with all of the interventions described in this book, defining specifically what you expect your child to do is crucial to avoiding misunderstandings or arguments. Also, having a specific definition of what constitutes planning will allow you to set clear goals and to monitor your child's progress. Below are some definitions of planning ahead that have been used in research with this intervention. Note that in the examples below, "1 day in advance" or "1 week in advance" refers to when your child records the information in his planner relative to when the test is actually scheduled to take place or when the project is due. For example, if on Tuesday your child's teacher announces that there will be a test on Friday and your child records that information, that qualifies as "at least 1 day in advance" (it is actually 4 days in advance). In addition, research with the planning intervention has shown that children need to record upcoming tests or projects in their planners on the date the test will occur or be due. In the example above, that means the child would record "Test today" in the Friday slot of that week, rather than in the Tuesday slot (the day the teacher announced the test). Children who record the information in the slot of the day the test/project is announced often forget about it as the week progresses (i.e., children rarely look backwards in their planners).

1. Recorded an upcoming test or quiz in her planner at least 1 day in advance, in general terms (e.g., Test today in math).
2. Recorded an upcoming test or quiz in her planner at least 1 day in advance, in specific terms (e.g., Test today in math, on multiplication; chapters 1–3).
3. Recorded that he would study for an upcoming test at least 1 day in advance of the test (e.g., Study for science test today).

4. Recorded that he would study for an upcoming test at least 1 day in advance and recorded the amount of time he would study (e.g., Study 30 minutes for science test today).

5. Recorded that he would study for an upcoming test at least 1 day in advance and recorded the study method (e.g., Study for science test today by making 20 flashcards).

6. Recorded that he would study for an upcoming test at least 1 day in advance and recorded the amount of time to study and method (e.g., Study for science today by making 20 flashcards and reviewing them for 30 minutes).

7. Recorded an upcoming project at least 1 week in advance of the project due date (e.g., Paper on Martin Luther King Jr. due today).

8. Recorded in general terms a specific day to work on a project or paper at least 1 day in advance of the due date (e.g., Work on MLK paper today).

9. Recorded a specific day to work on a project at least 1 day in advance of the due date and listed a specific activity (e.g., Research MLK on computer and take notes).

10. Broke down a project into at least two separate tasks and assigned separate dates for each activity (e.g., Research MLK on computer today and take notes, and on a later date in the planner, Write first draft of MLK paper today).

You probably noticed that in each of the above definitions the planning skills get progressively more complex. Having examples of definitions with increasing levels of detail allows you to start the intervention by setting realistic, achievable goals, as discussed in Chapter 2 (e.g., "This week I would like you to write down one upcoming test in your planner). You can then build on your child's success by having her complete more complex planning tasks (e.g., "Last week you did a great job recording a test in advance. This week I would like you to pick a time to study for a test and record that information in your planner"). Having these specific definitions will also allow you to use the point system and reward menu as described in Chapter 2, with the number of points your child earns varying depending on the complexity of the skill. For example, recording a test at least 1 day in advance might be worth two points in your system, whereas designating a specific time to study and what study method to use might be worth five points.

When you first begin this intervention with your child, you will need to walk her through the process of creating a study or work completion plan and show her exactly what you want her to do. Share the specific definitions (provided above) with your child and then use her school planner and currently assigned work to provide some examples of what would need to be recorded to meet each definition. Below is a script of how you might introduce and explain the planning intervention to your child. The example focuses on introducing planning ahead for tests and quizzes and random point values are included in the example. Remember that you can use any point values you want for each planning behavior or definition, depending on how you structure the rewards on your reward menu.

You have been doing really well with consistently recording your homework assignments and tests in your school planner. I want to challenge you a bit to see if you can also use your planner to make sure you are well prepared for your tests and quizzes ahead of time, so that we don't have to scramble as much at the last minute. You will have the opportunity to earn a lot more points to put toward your reward menu by using your planner to prepare in advance for tests and quizzes. How does that sound?

There are six ways that you can earn points for recording information about tests and quizzes in your planner. Each of the ways you can earn points is listed on this paper. Let's look at this first definition, which says, "Recorded an upcoming test or quiz in planner at least 1 day in advance." Let's say that on Monday your teacher tells you that on Wednesday you will have a math test. If you go into your planner and in the Wednesday math space write "Math test today," you would meet this definition and earn two points. If instead of just writing "Math test today," you recorded what the test covered ("Math test today on chapter 6"), you would meet the second definition on this sheet and earn three points. If you did that for both science and math class, you would earn six points!

The next few definitions on this sheet have to do with how you are planning to study for tests and quizzes. For example, if your math test was on Wednesday and in the Tuesday math space in your planner you wrote "Study for math test," you would earn four points. Writing that you are going to study really shows me that you are planning ahead for the test. If you also record the amount of time that you are going to study for the test, you will earn five points. For example, let's say that on Monday, you put in your planner that you have a math test on Wednesday and that it is on chapter 6. Then, in the Tuesday box in your planner your also write "Study 30 minutes for math test." You would earn three points for recording when your test is and what it will cover and another five points for recording that you will study and how much time you will study.

The next definition is similar except that instead of writing how much you are going to study, you would record how you are going to study. Can you give me an example of a method someone might use for studying? [Possible answers are read over notes, read over the chapters the test covers, make flashcards.] Very good! What is the method you usually use to study for tests? Sticking with our math test example, if you wrote "Make flashcards for math test" or "Outline chapter 6 for math test," you would earn six points.

To meet the last definition on this sheet, you would need to write both how much time you are going to study and the method of studying you are going to use (we'll call this your study plan). You would earn seven points for doing both. The nice thing about showing me that you can plan ahead like this is that you can earn points really fast. If you met the last definition on this sheet for all four of your classes (math, language arts, history, and science), you would earn 28 points in one day! Do you have any questions?

Let's go ahead and practice planning ahead for tests and quizzes now. We can work through the process of planning for one of your upcoming tests together. We can even go ahead and assign you points for practicing the skill with me. How does that sound?

OK, so you have a test on [day]. How much time would you normally study for a [subject] test? It is important that you be honest with me so that we can set a realistic goal for studying for this next test. OK, so you would normally study [X] minutes for a test like this. Is that how much you would like to study this time? OK, so you want to study [X] minutes for this test. When would you like to do that? OK, so go ahead and record in your planner that you would like to study on [X] day and record how many minutes you plan to study. Great. You already earned five points for doing that, plus what you earned for recording the test. If you wanted to earn more than five points, what would you need to do? You can look at these definitions if you want. That's right. If you recorded the method you are going to use to study (basically, how you are going to study), you would earn more points. How do you usually study for tests? Does that work well for you? OK, let's record the method you are going to use for this test in your planner. Great. Now you have earned seven points! Do you have any questions about what we just did? If you record that type of information in your planner every time your teacher tells you about a test, quiz, paper, or project, you will earn more points. I am going to check your planner each day after school to see if you have recorded any of this information and earned points.

You may want to walk your child through the process of breaking up tests and projects into smaller pieces a few more times to ensure that he completely understands. It is often helpful to slowly transfer responsibility for planning ahead to the child. For example, during the second week you might prompt the child by asking questions like, "I see you recorded a math test for Friday. Great job! Is there anything you would like to add to your planner about studying so you can earn more points? You can go record how you plan to study for the test and then bring your planner back to me to review if you want." It may take a few weeks of this type of prompting before the child can accomplish these tasks independently. You may want to discuss with your child the best time for him to record this information in his planner. Your child may not have enough time during the school day to think through a study plan and may need to establish a regular routine or schedule for recording study plans outside of school (e.g., he comes home and immediately puts study plans into the planner while having a snack).

LONG-TERM VIEW

In the first step of this intervention, parents simply get their child used to recording a plan for studying in her school planner. The intervention up to this point has not talked about whether the child's plan is a good one or if it will lead to a good grade. As your child gets used to recording a few details consistently (e.g., studying in advance, using what method, for how long), then you can begin to discuss improving his study plan. Also, you have been learning that how you implement the interventions with your child makes a difference in whether or not he is motivated to continue implementing the skills. For example, if the first time your child independently creates a study plan and brings you the planner you say "What!? There is no way that studying 20 minutes will be sufficient," you can pretty much guarantee that he will stop bringing you study plans. As outlined in Chapter 2, your child will experience more success if you focus on positively reinforcing his attempts to learn new skills, in this case learning time management by creating a study plan. The next step is shaping the study plan.

Once you are ready help your child start shaping study plans, try doing so primarily by asking questions rather than by telling your child what to do. Simply put, adolescents do not like to be told what to do and are likely to resist whatever they are directly told to do, even if it is the best idea in the world. Therefore try to make modifying your child's study plan (e.g., more studying) sound like his idea. For example, "I see you are going to study math for 20 minutes on Thursday. Great job recording that in your planner. Is that similar to your study plan for your last math test? Did you end up following that plan pretty well? How did you feel it worked for you? Is there anything you would like to do differently this time?"

Another way to approach improving your child's study plan is to set specific goals for each test or quiz, such as the grade that he wants to receive, and then to evaluate the study plan relative to the goal. "You got a C on your last math test, which is pretty good. What grade would you like to shoot for on this next test? Okay, a B. Have you thought about making any changes to your study plan this time around?" It is important that, early in this process, you acknowledge that all study plans require work and that this is true for everyone. Set the expectation that your child will most likely not reach his goal on the first try and tell him that this is normal. You can even make it seem a bit like a game, or describe it as a scientific process. "There are so many factors that go into doing well on a test, including how you study (the method), how long you study, how many times you study, and how far in advance you start studying. Let's approach this scientifically and manipulate these factors one at a time until we find the best combination." The next step in the process is to help your child begin to think about when during the day and evening he is going to accomplish all of the tasks he has outlined in the study plan. This question is addressed in the managing time and balancing responsibilities intervention described in the next chapter.

Chapter 7

Managing Time and Balancing Responsibilities

SUMMARY OF THE INTERVENTION

The overall goals of the intervention are to:

- Help children learn to develop and implement a specific plan for balancing their school and extracurricular responsibilities.
- Gradually teach children how to accurately estimate how long activities will take to complete.

What is needed to implement this intervention?

- An evening schedule (such as the example provided in this chapter).
- A child who is consistently recording homework assignments and tests in a planner and has at least begun to break work completion into smaller pieces and to plan ahead for the completion of each task (as described in Chapter 6).

What is required of you, the parent?

- Willingness to work with your child to create an evening schedule, mapping out exactly when all after-school activities will take place and estimating how long they will last.
- Willingness to work patiently with your child to gradually teach her to more accurately estimate how long activities actually take.
- Willingness to establish a reward menu as outlined in Chapter 2 that will provide incentives for your child to complete evening schedules.

Developmental considerations:

- The same developmental considerations as listed in Chapter 6.

BACKGROUND

Many children and their families have very busy after-school schedules. As children move into middle and high school they often start participating in sports or club activities that involve lengthy practice sessions after school. Children also may choose to participate in a host of additional after-school activities, such as tutoring, after-school programs, karate, or music lessons. In middle and high school, children commonly do not arrive home until 5:00 or 6:00 p.m. Further, the school workload of assignments, tests, and so forth, can vary considerably from day to day. As such, it can be a significant family challenge to plan ahead and to find sufficient time to devote to homework and studying.

Families often find that evenings after a school day are quite stressful because everyone is rushing (e.g., to make and eat dinner, to prepare for the next day, and to complete work). Sometimes, the child's schoolwork simply cannot be completed before the ideal bedtime, and as a result, the child stays up late and is tired the next day. This can lead to a negative cycle in which the child is tired, irritable, and less efficient in her schoolwork the next day, and so again has to stay up late to complete her work. Tired children and stressed parents do not make a good combination, and when this is the case, discussions about work completion frequently end in arguments. Families often feel too busy to take the time to map out activities and develop a schedule for the week. Families that do plan weekly schedules sometimes are faced with the realization that they are committed to too many activities. The evening schedule intervention described in this chapter can be useful for teaching children to plan ahead. This intervention may also help families step back and reevaluate their commitments.

DESCRIPTION OF THE INTERVENTION

This intervention primarily involves making a detailed list of tasks to be completed by the child and putting those tasks into an after-school schedule that is broken down into 30-minute increments. Although this process sounds relatively simple, accurately estimating how long activities will take is a complex skill that is developed over time. Parents will need to work patiently with their children and be prepared for the first few evening schedules to not go exactly as planned. Figure 7.1 is an example of a completed evening schedule so that you can see what the end product looks like. The example is followed by a description of how to work with your child to develop and revise an evening schedule.

The first step in the process is identifying a good time to complete the evening schedule. The evening schedule obviously needs to be completed in advance (i.e., the child is planning ahead), but it can't be completed before the child knows exactly what tasks need to be accomplished. Some families prefer to complete the evening schedule the night before, other families like to complete the evening schedule first thing after the child arrives home from school. When you initially complete the evening schedule with your child, simply ask for his input and estimates of how long activities will take and do not challenge what he says. For example, if your child says that homework that evening will probably take 10 minutes but you suspect it will take 1 hour, you should not raise the issue at this point. You will help your child to gradually develop a more accurate evening schedule. The initial goal is simply to get your child to be willing to engage in this planning exercise with you. Below is an example of how you might introduce the evening schedule.

You have worked really hard at learning to break down your assignments and tests into smaller pieces and to plan ahead for the completion of each piece. I have been really impressed. One thing we haven't talked much about is your schedule after school each day. I have noticed that we are really busy these days. It seems like we spend most of our time driving around and you are not getting home until 5:30 most nights. I want us to work together to make sure that you have enough time after school to complete all of your work. Will you work with me on that?

FIGURE 7.1. Example Evening Schedule

Time	Activity	Notes
4:30	Snack	
5:00	Dance class	
5:30	Dance class	
6:00	Dinner	
6:30	Dinner	
7:00	Complete science homework	Answer questions in the textbook at the end of chapter 6.
7:30	Complete science homework	Finish answering chapter 6 questions.
8:00	TV	
8:30	TV	
9:00	Study spelling words	Make flashcards from spelling list on page 76 and review cards for 15 minutes.
9:30	Shower	
10:00	Bed	

This evening schedule sheet is designed to help us plan our afternoons and evenings on particularly busy days. As an example, let's use this evening schedule to plan your day after school today. I am going to write in your responses this time.

What time will you get home from school today? What will you do first? How long do you think that will take? What will you do after that? How long do you think that will take? What time do we usually eat dinner? How long do you think we typically spend eating dinner? What will you do after dinner? What time do you plan on going to bed?

Great, tomorrow let's remember to talk about how it went. We can see how accurate we were in guessing how long each activity would take. Then we can make adjustments and see if we can develop better and more accurate plans. How does that sound? Once we get the hang of this, I will start giving you points toward your reward menu for completing evening schedules on your own and showing them to me. What do you think, maybe 10 points per evening schedule?

The next day you should meet with your child to review the completed evening schedule and to discuss how accurate the time estimates were. Below are a few suggestions to engage your child in this discussion. Start generally, asking open-ended questions such as, "How did it go? Did anything unexpected come up?" Then produce a copy of the evening schedule and review each of the activities listed, step by step. You can ask questions such as, "You estimated that you would get home around 5:30. What time did you get home? You thought that it would take 10 minutes to complete the homework and that you would get it done before dinner. When did you complete that homework and how long did it take?"

You obviously will be aware of inconsistencies between what was recorded and what actually happened. You can gently prompt your child to make revisions and can even continue to use the term "we" to make sure it doesn't sound as if you are blaming your child for getting it wrong. For example, "Wow, we were really off there. We thought that we would get done with dinner at 6:30 and we were not done until 7:15." Or "I see homework took 2 hours instead of 1 hour. I didn't see that coming. Do you think homework usually takes closer to 2 hours?" Once the evening schedule has been reviewed, you and your child should work together to create a new evening schedule, applying what you both just learned to make it more accurate. An example script is provided below for helping your child revise the evening schedule.

You did a nice job planning your activities after school using the evening schedule. Some things went exactly as we planned, and other things didn't work out the way we thought they would. I would like to work with you to create another evening schedule to plan your after-school activities today. We can use what we learned from creating the first schedule to make this one even better.

You ended up completing your homework right before bed instead of before dinner as you had planned. Do you think it's better to finish homework before dinner? What are the benefits of completing homework right before bed? Is completing homework before dinner something that you would like to try to accomplish today after school? Okay, let's write that on your evening schedule. What could you do to remind yourself to start working on homework before dinner?

You estimated 10 minutes to complete homework on your last evening schedule. From what you said, it sounds as if it took closer to an hour. Did you underestimate the time it would take or did something get in the way of you finishing quickly? It can be hard to estimate how long homework might take. Maybe you could block off 1 hour every night and plan for that in your evening schedule. If it takes you less than an hour you can either get in some extra work or you can have extra free time. What do you think? How much time would you like to schedule for homework today after school?

LONG-TERM VIEW

The ultimate goal of this intervention is for the child to start developing accurate evening schedules on her own and to bring those to the parent for review. The parent then provides the child with points for taking the time to plan after-school activities. Many options can be used for rewarding the child with points, but regardless of the option chosen, it is important to provide the child with a set number of points simply for making the effort (for completing a schedule on her own). The parent can also offer additional bonus points for the level of detail or for accuracy. For example, when your child uses the second column to state specifically what activities he is going to complete in a certain time slot, you would give him bonus points. Bonus points also can be given if your child sticks to his evening schedule and completes all of his work by a designated time.

If your child is consistently staying up past his bedtime despite doing his best to plan after-school activities, you are left with two choices. The first choice is to help your child learn to work more efficiently by focusing and staying on task, as described in Chapter 4. For example, many families rely on flashcards because they can be taken and reviewed anywhere (e.g., to a sibling's swim meet), so studying is more portable. The second choice is to reevaluate the number of activities your child is committed to participating in each day after school. What often happens is that activities that were fairly easily completed in prior years (soccer, music lessons, and tutoring) are suddenly no longer feasible because the child's workload increases steadily throughout middle and high school. This can lead to difficult choices about what activities take priority. However, having to adjust for overcommitment can offer another important planning and time management lesson that you can teach your child. That is, sometimes we can't do everything we want to, and we have to learn to prioritize. In the long term, some families prefer to have their children complete evening schedules every day because they find it helpful. Other families only use the evening schedule when the after-school period is feeling rushed and stressful, and they want to monitor what is going on in order to make informed choices.

Putting It All Together

Chapter 8

Collaboration: Working With Your Child's School

WHY INVOLVE THE SCHOOL?

None of the interventions described in this book require school involvement. In fact, all of the HOPS interventions, with the exception of teacher initials, could be implemented without the school being aware that a family is working with their child. However, many parents find that involving the school helps them adhere to the FAMILY guiding principles discussed in detail in Chapter 2. Those principles are listed below, followed by a brief description of how the school might help you to address each principle.

Feasibility

Providing effective interventions is hard work for parents. Start small so that you can implement the intervention exactly the way you intended. If you work with your child's school to implement the HOPS interventions, a teacher, school counselor, or school psychologist may be willing to share the burden of implementation. For example, you might complete an organizational skills checklist once a week and a school counselor could complete the checklist a second time each week. This intervention plan would significantly reduce the amount of monitoring you needed to complete each week and would therefore make the intervention more feasible for you to implement. In addition, meeting with your child's school prior to providing the intervention will allow you to start small by picking the most important behavior to target first. Your child's teachers may have a unique perspective on which HOPS behavior is the most important for your child's academic success (e.g., homework recording versus organization). Identifying the behavior that is most important from the teacher's perspective can help you prioritize and determine where to start.

Achievable Goals

To ensure that your child has some success early in the intervention process, set easy-to-achieve goals for him. You can always raise the bar later. Seeking school involvement can help because most of the HOPS interventions target behaviors that, at least partly, take place in the school setting. Therefore it will be difficult to set achievable goals without first gathering input from your child's teachers. For example, let's say you wanted to focus on reducing the number of assignments your child fails to turn in each week. To set a realistic goal (e.g., no more than two missing assignments), you would need your child's teachers to look back in their gradebooks and tell you what is typical (e.g., the average number of assignments your child has missed per week). Likewise, if you wanted to set goals for how much time your child takes to complete his homework (i.e., completing work more efficiently), you would first need to know how long your child's teachers expect the work to take (i.e., what is the norm across students in the teacher's class). Finally, if you wanted to implement the teacher initials intervention, you would first need to know how many teachers were willing to sign; otherwise you might set a goal that is impossible for your child to reach.

Monitoring and Rewarding

The intervention simply will not work if your child's progress with homework, organization, and planning skills is not consistently and frequently monitored and rewarded. By working with your child's school, you may be able to monitor your child's implementation of the HOPS skills on a more frequent and consistent basis. For example, if your work schedule dictates that you can monitor only 1 day per week after school (e.g., you don't get home early enough on the other nights), the school might agree to complete the checklist two additional times, significantly increasing the likelihood that the intervention will work. Alternatively, you might be able to target multiple HOPS behaviors at the same time if the school agreed to monitor and reward one behavior (e.g., organization) while you focused on monitoring and rewarding a different behavior (e.g., homework recording). Finally, having rewards available in two different settings—that is, your child earning points at home and at school—will significantly increase the potential that the rewards will be meaningful and thereby increase your child's motivation to implement the HOPS skills.

Intervention Should Be Fun

The tone you set with your child when explaining why you are implementing an intervention and describing how it will work is very important. Set a positive tone, making it clear that this is an opportunity for him to earn praise and rewards. School involvement can help because school counselors and psychologists receive training and lots of practice with introducing interventions in a positive manner and with reinforcing children's successes. Accordingly, they will be able to reinforce the positive message you present when you introduce HOPS. If your child is hearing positive messages from multiple people, he will be more likely to believe them and to be willing to try the new system.

Letting Go

Picking your battles, focusing on your child's successes, and temporarily letting go of the other concerns you have about your child's behavior will make the intervention process go more smoothly. Your child's school can help with this effort too. Letting go of some concerns (e.g., your child's behavior problems in the classroom) in order to focus on improving other areas (e.g., homework recording) can be very difficult. However, this may be easier if you know that the school is monitoring and providing interventions for other important behaviors that you are temporarily letting go of.

You

You, the parent, are a critical piece of the puzzle. You need to monitor your own stress level and seek help if necessary to ensure that personal issues do not get in the way of your child's success. Sometimes parents are simply under too much stress to provide their child with the HOPS interventions without getting angry or emotional. In those circumstances, having the child's school involved can be important because parents can rely on others, such as a school psychologist, to implement the interventions and to provide constructive feedback about the child's academic progress.

WHAT SCHOOL INVOLVEMENT MIGHT LOOK LIKE

Schools can be involved with HOPS at many different levels. The discussion below addresses three potential ways that parents could collaborate with their child's school.

Assessment

At a minimum, parents should involve the school in the HOPS assessment process. Specifically, parents should request a meeting with their child's teachers, counselors, and school psychologist to gather information about what behaviors are viewed as most critical to their child's academic success. This type of a meeting will help to identify the most important behaviors to target with the HOPS intervention. If the school is not already involved with HOPS interventions, in this meeting, you can provide a brief outline of the HOPS interventions and the various options for where you might want to start. You can then seek the input of those attending the meeting. Teachers can often be helpful in providing a developmental perspective on your child's behaviors. Specifically, teachers have the benefit of seeing not just your child but many children the same age or grade as your child. This may allow them to comment on how your child's behavior compares with the behavior of his peers in the class. For example, you might feel that organization is a significant problem, but the teacher might note that your child's organizational skills are actually pretty similar to those of his classmates.

Once you and your child's teachers have reached an understanding on what specific behavior to target, you should provide a more detailed overview of what the chosen HOPS intervention will consist of. You can ask whether anyone has any questions or concerns. For example, you might explain the rationale behind the teacher initials intervention or the HOPS single binder system and solicit input. This provides teachers and others with an opportunity to suggest modifications to the interventions to make them more workable in their classrooms. This way, when you introduce the intervention to your child, you can state with confidence that his teachers are glad to help.

How the School Supports the Parent

Many times, the assessment meeting will be the extent of school involvement with the HOPS intervention. Sometimes, however, schools are already using HOPS or will receive the parents' information about HOPS enthusiastically and ask how they can help. Accordingly, prior to the assessment meeting you should give some thought to how the school might support your intervention efforts so that you are ready to discuss options. One way the school can support you with HOPS is by taking on some of the monitoring responsibilities. The level of monitoring the school provides can be very small but still be of significant help. For example, one of your child's teachers might agree to complete an organizational skills checklist once each week. Alternatively, one of your child's teachers might agree to spend 5 minutes with him at the beginning of each week to help him plan ahead for the upcoming week's academic tasks. For example, the teacher might help your child develop a study plan for an upcoming test and record the tasks to be accomplished in the school planner. Simply having another adult monitoring your child's behavior consistently will increase the likelihood of success, even if the school does not establish a formal reward menu.

How the Parent Supports the School

The greatest level of involvement occurs when the school takes primary responsibility for implementing the HOPS intervention and the parent plays a supportive role. As described in the Preface, many schools already use the HOPS intervention, and the school may have approached you about implementing HOPS rather than vice versa. If the school is implementing HOPS, this typically means that they will be meeting with your child in a small-group format one time each week to teach her the HOPS skills and to reward her progress. In these cases, it is critical that you offer to support the school by monitoring and by providing additional reward options. School counselors and psychologists typically serve many students, and as such, it is unlikely that they will have the time to monitor your child's behavior (e.g., complete checklists) more than once a week. In those situations, you can offer to complete the checklist on a different day to increase the frequency of monitoring. Similarly, school counselors and psychologists have limited budgets and may have a difficult time offering multiple meaningful reward options for the reward menu. If this is true at your child's school, it is very important that you offer to meet with the interventionist to suggest reward options that you can implement at home (e.g., privileges such as TV and cell phone time). A reward menu that is developed collaboratively in this manner will contain more meaningful reward options, significantly increasing the child's motivation to implement the HOPS skills.

GENERAL GUIDELINES FOR APPROACHING THE SCHOOL

The parent–school relationship shares many similarities with the parent–child relationship discussed in this book. For example, this book talks repeatedly about the importance of being positive and about introducing new interventions as opportunities for children. This book also talks about setting up interventions that are feasible and about establishing achievable goals. All of these principles are equally important when you are talking with your child's school about his academic progress and asking them to support you in providing services for your child.

Unfortunately, it is quite common for parents to have a negative relationship with their child's school. Parents may feel that the school has not provided enough support in the past or that the school is identifying their child's problems but not providing viable solutions. It is very difficult for parents to continually watch their child struggling at school, and this can lead to feelings of frustration and animosity. Sometimes, parents get so frustrated with the school that they have difficulty staying calm and controlling their emotions during school meetings. Parents in this situation are often unable to accomplish the goals they set out to achieve with the meeting.

When you meet with the school to discuss your child's academic progress and the HOPS interventions, present your desires positively. Describe the HOPS interventions you want to implement and emphasize how much work you will be doing at home to improve your child's academic performance. This type of a message has a much better chance of being well received. During the meeting, stay focused on what you would like to see happen in implementing the HOPS intervention and try to avoid bringing up additional issues and concerns. Also, make sure that what you are asking of the school is reasonable and be prepared to present multiple reasonable options for how the school might be able to support your child. Teachers are much more likely to be receptive to ideas when they are given the opportunity to choose which plan will work best for them. Just like working with your child, you want the school to take on only as much work as will allow them to be successful.

Remember that how you present your message is important. If you know that you will have difficulty remaining calm and presenting HOPS in a logical, feasible, and positive way, you could bring an outside person to the meeting to help represent you. This could be a professional such as an advocate or a psychologist, or it could be a family member who is less emotionally involved in your relationship with the school. Meet with this person ahead of time to outline what you would like to see accomplished during the meeting. It may also be helpful to give the outside person permission to redirect you or to calm you down by putting a hand on your shoulder or some other agreed-upon gesture. The most critical thing to remember is that the purpose of the meeting is to help your child, and you simply cannot accomplish that goal in a meeting filled with arguments and accusations.

Chapter 9

Examples of Successful Intervention Systems

GOALS OF THIS CHAPTER

This chapter provides two real-life examples of successful HOPS interventions. In these examples, parents can learn how to troubleshoot and adjust their methods when interventions are not going as planned.

EXAMPLE 1—TEACHER INITIALS AND ORGANIZATION

John is halfway through his sixth-grade year of school. In his district, students make the transition to middle school after the completion of fifth grade. He performed fairly well in elementary school, achieving A's and B's during the final semester of his fifth-grade year. John's parents are divorced, and he lives with his mother Sunday through Wednesday and with his father Thursday through Saturday. During his fifth-grade year, John started missing homework assignments (failing to complete them or to turn them in) more frequently than in past years. He had always missed assignments occasionally, but in fifth grade his parents found that they had to stay in frequent contact with teachers or John would forget to complete work. He also occasionally lost his homework (e.g., worksheets) between home and school. This trend worsened following the transition to middle school. John simply could not remember all of the assignments he had to complete each day now that he had four separate teachers. He sometimes wrote down his assignments in a planner but not consistently. He also continued to lose assignments. John's parents noticed that his bookbag was full of papers, and they often found themselves searching through the bookbag for his assignments and graded work. John received one C and one D on his first semester report card, the first time he had received a grade below a B.

John's mother scheduled a meeting with the school psychologist, school counselor, and teachers to discuss John's difficulties with assignment completion. The school psychologist noted that they were implementing the HOPS intervention program at the school. They currently did not have any open slots in the HOPS group but suggested that she try implementing the HOPS teacher initials and the binder and bookbag organization interventions. The school psychologist talked briefly with John's mother about how to establish a point system and a reward menu. The psychologist noted that if John's difficulties continued, he would be enrolled in the HOPS group at the beginning of his seventh-grade year.

John's mother read about the interventions and introduced them to John. Next, they established a reward menu together. During the next week, John's mom checked his planner each day after school. He received two teacher initials each day of the week but never more than two (four teacher initials were expected, one from each core class teacher). On the reward system, John had to receive all four initials to earn a reward for the day, and so John did not receive any rewards. He spent the remainder of the week with his father. When he returned to his mother's house the following week, she saw that he had not received any teacher initials during the second half of the week. John expressed that he didn't like getting initials and wanted to stop. John's mom took the opportunity to reread Chapter 2 of the HOPS book and identified two potential problems. First, John was not achieving his goals and therefore was not receiving any rewards, and second, John's homework planner was not being monitored consistently because John's father had not been told about the intervention.

In terms of organization, John's mother had completed the organizational skills checklist one time during the week and found that John was not really using the homework folder as intended. Although she helped him fix his homework folder, she did not press the issue (i.e., no lengthy conversations about why he wasn't using it correctly); instead, she chose to concentrate on troubleshooting teacher initials.

John's mother met with John and talked to him about the teacher initials system. She remained positive and praised him for getting two initials each day during the time that he was staying with her. She stated that she wanted to reward him for his efforts and they revised the reward menu so that John could earn extra TV and video game time for getting two initials out of four. He also could earn a bonus reward (an additional choice from of the menu) for each additional initial he received. He seemed excited about this change but expressed that he was hesitant about asking his math teacher, who scares him, to initial. John's mother decided she would e-mail the math teacher, explain the rationale for the teacher initials system, make sure the teacher knew it was temporary, and emphasize that it is John's responsibility to ask for initials. The teacher responded that he would sign only if John brought his planner up at the end of class with the homework already recorded. John's mother conveyed this information to John. She also called his father and explained the initials system. John's father stated that he was willing to check the planner after school and asked for a copy of the reward menu.

The next week, John averaged between two and four initials each day and was consistently able to choose one or two rewards daily from his reward menu. John and his mother then met to discuss strategies that might help John get all four initials every day. John stated that he meant to get all four teacher initials but kept forgetting. They decided to tape an index card to the outside of his binder with the instruction "Get initials" written on it. They also wrote the same instruction on the top of every page in his planner, and taped a note saying "Get initials" to the outside of his pencil and pen holder (all the places he was most likely to see during class). John's mom also raised the bar slightly so that John had to receive at least three initials to earn a reward from the reward menu and communicated this change to his father.

The following week John received either three or four initials every day of the week. His mother decided not to make any further changes to the initials system but instead decided to begin working on John's organization system. John and his mother discussed why he was having trouble maintaining the homework folder. He stated that he simply didn't have time during class to file all of the papers in their appropriate places (e.g., homework in homework folder and completed work moved to the appropriate class sections). His mother suggested that they establish a specific time for him to move completed papers from the homework folder into the appropriate sections of his binder after school. She said that she would remind him the first few days and then after that he would be expected to remember on his own to organize his binder. They put signs on the refrigerator as visual prompts. They decided that on Monday and Thursday John would spend 10 minutes organizing his binder and bookbag immediately when he got home from school. His mother indicated that she would check his binder and bookbag each Monday evening and would ask his father to check each Thursday evening. John's mother initially helped John organize his materials to make sure he knew what was expected and then gradually reduced the assistance she was providing. By the third week, John was consistently remembering to clean out his binder and bookbag twice each week after school. He was earning full points on the organization checklist and continued to receive three or four teacher initials every day. John's mother planned to move to Phase 2 of the teacher initials system (random checks with the teacher and no initials requirement) the following week.

EXAMPLE 2—TIME MANAGEMENT AND PLANNING

Liza is in the ninth grade, her first year of high school. She did well throughout middle school, earning mostly A's and B's on her report cards. She is active in the school band and is on the debate team. Although she did well during her eighth-grade year, it was a very stressful year for the family (she lives with her mother, father, and younger brother). The family felt like they were constantly rushing and almost always running behind, and found that they were arguing frequently. In addition, Liza's parents had hoped that she would take more responsibility for her academic achievement in high school and that they could provide less support for homework completion and planning activities. However, Liza's parents were continuing to provide a high level of support and felt that if they reduced their support, Liza would not be able to maintain her current grade point average of 3.4. Liza's parents did an Internet search for resources related to time management and planning strategies and found the HOPS book. They decided to try implementing the time management, planning, and evening schedule interventions. Liza's father also thought that the organization system seemed like a good idea and suggested that they switch her to a one-binder system. He noted that while she wasn't currently losing papers, it could become a problem when she transitioned to college, and he wanted to encourage good organization habits.

Liza's parents met with her and explained the new systems. They showed her how to break assignments into small pieces and to record them in her planner and how to complete an evening schedule by transferring the tasks from her planner into the evening schedule form. They also helped her take all of her materials from the four binders she was currently using (one for each class) and transfer them into a single 3-inch D-ring binder. Liza was not happy about all of the changes and complained a great deal. Her parents told her that if she tried hard with the new systems she would be able to earn rewards. They said that she could earn money to go to a movie on the weekends with her friends. They also said that if she did really well with the new systems she could get a new cell phone.

The following week, Liza wrote down her assignments in more detail and planned out study activities in advance of a social studies test. She also completed one evening schedule. Her parents found that they were too busy to monitor her implementation of the HOPS skills as frequently as they had planned. At the end of the week, Liza asked for her money to go the movies. Her father stated that she didn't earn money for the movies because she only created one evening schedule and developed a study plan for only one test. Liza was furious and argued with her parents. In the end, they decided that she had done enough and gave her money to go to the movies.

The following week Liza's mother did not monitor (complete checklists) on Monday or Tuesday, but she remembered to complete the checklists on Wednesday. However, when she checked, Liza had not completed any evening schedules and had recorded her homework but had not broken tasks down into steps. Liza stated that she hated the new organization system and refused to use it anymore. She stated that having one large binder made her "look weird" and that kids teased her. Her parents were angry with her for not using the HOPS skills and told her that she did not earn a movie with friends that weekend and that she was not on the "right path" for earning a cell phone. Liza was furious and ran up to her room and slammed the door. She yelled that she was done with the system.

Her parents decided to give up on the HOPS systems because they were not working. Over the next 2 months the situation at home worsened. Arguments were happening more frequently, and Liza almost always had to stay up until midnight to complete her homework. As a result, she was exhausted and irritable during the day. Liza's parents decided to seek outside support and scheduled an appointment with a child psychologist. They brought the HOPS manual to the meeting to show the psychologist what they had tried.

The psychologist asked them if they would be willing to try the interventions again with a few small changes. She suggested that they try the HOPS interventions again for 1 month and stated that if the systems were still not working, they would move on to a different intervention approach. For homework, the psychologist asked Liza's parents to read Chapter 2 of the manual, which they admitted to skimming the first time around. The psychologist asked them to identify three ways that they might implement the interventions differently this time.

Liza's parents took the homework seriously and asked themselves each of the questions associated with the FAMILY acronym, as described in the troubleshooting section at the end of Chapter 2. They came up with three changes that they wanted to make. First, they realized that they had not been monitoring consistently and felt that this was likely because they were trying to do too much. The family had a very busy schedule and they did not have enough time to complete each of the checklists daily. They decided to drop the organization intervention (binder system) because organization was less of a priority at the moment. They also made a commitment to monitor more consistently. Liza's parents created a schedule for themselves, listing who would be in charge of monitoring each day of the week and when monitoring would occur. Second, they felt that the rewards they had offered (a movie on the weekend and a new cell phone sometime) were too delayed, and they decided to switch to daily reward options. They also recognized that they had not established clear goals for exactly what Liza needed to accomplish to earn the rewards. They felt that the lack of specific goals had led to disagreements. In response, they came up with specific, realistic, and achievable goals for Liza to meet on a daily basis and wrote out privileges (e.g., 15 minutes using Mom's cell phone) that Liza could earn each day. And third, they felt that their own busy schedules and stress were preventing them from making the intervention fun and from keeping their conversations with Liza positive. They decided to bring this issue up with the psychologist.

Although Liza's parents had identified three good ways to improve the interventions, Liza was not at all interested in starting the system again given her previous bad experience. She refused to talk with her parents about starting to use the time management and planning strategies again. Liza's parents consulted with the child psychologist and they decided to bring Liza to the next session. The psychologist stated that sometimes having a third, independent party introduce a new system can help adolescents be more receptive. During the meeting, the psychologist emphasized the clear and realistic goals being suggested by Liza's parents. In addition, Liza's parents verbally took responsibility for the failure of the intervention the first time and told Liza that they were committed to being more consistent. Liza's parents also made sure to frame everything positively. Specifically, they did not talk about consequences, only the opportunity to earn points. They were also able to praise Liza during the session, acknowledging that she was already doing very well in school and that they were proud of her academic performance. Liza reluctantly agreed to give the interventions a second chance.

Liza's parents created a reward menu in which Liza earned points for each test she recorded at least 1 day in advance and extra points for recording when she would study for the test and for how long. Liza was able to earn privileges (e.g., cell phone time) daily rather than weekly but also had the option of saving her points for larger weekly rewards (e.g., movie with friends). Liza's parents consistently recorded the points Liza earned, remained consistent with their monitoring plan, and focused on the positive (Liza's successes). They continued working with the psychologist and, during sessions, role-played how to approach difficult issues with Liza. For example, they role-played working with Liza to refine her evening schedule to more accurately estimate the time that homework activities would take. By the end of the month, Liza was consistently breaking her projects, papers, and tests into smaller tasks and setting deadlines for herself in her planner. She did not always accomplish the tasks during the time she had planned (e.g., study when she said she would and for how long), but her parents chose to focus only on her progress when speaking with her about the interventions. Liza completed an evening schedule about two times a week on her own and was beginning to more accurately estimate how long homework would take. The evening schedule intervention made the family realize that there was simply not enough time after school for Liza to complete all of her scheduled extracurricular activities and her homework if she was going to get to bed by 10 p.m. They decided to discuss the issue of being overscheduled at the next session with the psychologist because they anticipated that Liza would not want to drop any of her extracurricular activities. Overall, Liza's parents were pleased that she had begun to independently demonstrate time management and planning skills and felt that she was better prepared for the transition to college.

Chapter 10

Choosing Next Steps

NEXT STEPS

This chapter discusses what you can do if you implement the HOPS interventions and find that your child is continuing to struggle academically.

ASSESSING THE PROBLEM

Many different factors contribute to a child's academic success. HOPS interventions address a variety of different behaviors, ranging from staying focused during work completion to using planning and time management skills. However, by no means does HOPS address all of the behaviors that are important for academic success. If you have implemented HOPS successfully and your child is still not reaching her academic potential, further evaluation may be warranted. Frequently, additional behaviors will need to be improved with other interventions before a child can reach his full academic potential. Alternatively, assessment may reveal that your expectations for your child's academic performance or progress are not realistic. Either way, assessment is a useful tool for deciding on next steps.

Figure 10.1 lists some of the many reasons why children struggle academically. You may find it helpful to work through this list by identifying the areas you believe are currently hindering your child's academic success as well as the areas you would like to learn more about. This is by no means a comprehensive list. This list is simply intended to serve as a guide for identifying behaviors that could benefit from further assessment.

Once you have identified the behaviors that you believe are impeding your child's academic success and the behaviors you would like to learn more about, the next step is to obtain a formal assessment of those behaviors. Assessment is important because determining whether behaviors are normative or problematic can be difficult. Specifically, all children engage in the behaviors listed in Figure 10.1 at some level, and engaging in these behaviors does not necessarily indicate a problem. A formal assessment provides information on how your child is functioning relative to his peers. Often parents learn from the assessment process that behaviors that seemed problematic are actually normal for children that age. That is important information to have because it can help you adjust your expectations for your child. Alternatively, the assessment may reveal that your child is

FIGURE 10.1. Behaviors Associated With Academic Success

Behavior	Your Response **Yes** (definitely a concern), **Unsure** (maybe, need more information), or **No** (not a concern)
Math ability: • The child is performing below grade level in math. For example, the class has moved on to division, but the child still has not mastered multiplication.	
Reading ability: • The child is performing below grade level in reading. For example, the child reads slower than his peers or has difficulty with reading comprehension.	
Writing ability: • The child's writing may not be legible (e.g., handwriting problem) or the child may have significant problems with organization of writing compared with his peers.	
Study skills: • The child's study methods are not effective. The child studies for sufficient amounts of time but still does not fully understand or cannot recall the material when necessary.	
Note-taking skills: • The child is expected to take notes and fails to do so or is unsure of what information to record. Class notes end up being difficult to use for studying.	
Focus in the classroom: • The child is off task in the classroom more often than peers. Child daydreams or fails to pay attention and, as a result, does not complete classwork or does not understand the material that was presented.	
Disruptive behavior in the classroom: • The child talks to peers too frequently or at inappropriate times during class. The child acts out during class to get classmates' attention.	
Depression, sadness, or apathy: • The child seems to feel negative about most aspects of school. The child does not like school and demonstrates very little motivation to try to do better.	
Anxiety or worry: • The child expresses worries about her academic performance, and these worries may interfere with sleep or with her ability to recall information when taking tests.	
Interpersonal and social functioning: • The child is having difficulty making or maintaining friendships or has a peer group that is a negative influence.	

significantly behind his peers in one or more areas, and this information would help you determine what type of intervention is needed.

How you pursue further assessment depends on the behavior you are interested in learning more about. For the first five behaviors on the list (math through note taking), your child's school psychologist is typically the best place to start. School psychologists are responsible for completing psychoeducational evaluations. These evaluations essentially assess how your child is performing academically relative to his peers and relative to his intellectual capacity. If you do not have a school psychologist at your child's school, then a child psychologist can also complete a psychoeducational evaluation. For the next two behaviors on the list (focus and disruptive behaviors), your child's pediatrician is a good place to start. Pediatricians are trained to evaluate these problems and can make recommendations for treatment. If your pediatrician is not comfortable providing an assessment for these issues, you can seek an evaluation from a child psychologist. The last three behaviors on the list (depression, anxiety, and interpersonal) should be evaluated by a child psychologist. The psychologist will be able to tell you whether your child has clinically significant problems in any of those areas and if he or she meets criteria for a mood disorder diagnosis. The child psychologist will also be able to make treatment recommendations.

Regardless of the next steps that you choose for your child, the most important ideas to take from this book are the FAMILY guiding principles, because they will continue to apply. If you can remain positive with your child, focus on successes, and continue to set realistic and achievable goals, the intervention process will go more smoothly and be more successful.

Index

T

tasks, list of, 46
teacher initials system, 24–25
    example, 55–57
    implementation, 25
    introducing, 25–26
    long-term view, 26
    monitoring collection of, 25
teachers
    collaborating with, 25
    input, 9
tests, 40
    breaking into smaller pieces, 43–44
time management intervention, 9, 45–48
    example, 57–59
    long-term view, 48
    summary, 45
tone, positive, 52
trends, detecting, 16
troubleshooting, 18–19

W

working efficiently, 48

Y

you, 18, 19
    school involvement, 52